3/92   14⁰⁰

reduced

9⁹⁵

INDIAN CIVILIZATION
The Formative Period

INDIAN CIVILIZATION

The Formative Period

A STUDY OF ARCHAEOLOGY AS ANTHROPOLOGY

S.C. MALIK

INDIAN INSTITUTE OF ADVANCED STUDY
SHIMLA

MOTILAL BANARSIDASS
DELHI VARANASI PATNA MADRAS

First Edition 1968
Reprinted 1987

© Indian Institute of Advanced Study 1968

Published by the Secretary for
INDIAN INSTITUTE OF ADVANCED STUDY
Rashtrapati Nivas, Shimla 171005

in association with

MOTILAL BANARSIDASS
Bungalow Road, Jawahar Nagar, Delhi 110007

Branches

Chowk, Varanasi 221001
Ashok Rajpath, Patna 800004
120 Royapettah High Road, Mylapore, Madras 600004

ISBN: 81-208-0328-0

Printed in India
by Pramodh Kapur at Raj Bandhu Industrial Co.,
C-61, Mayapuri Industrial Area, Phase II, New Delhi 110064

To

MY PARENTS

FOREWORD

Since in his Introduction Dr. S. C. Malik provides an adequate explanation of what he proposes to do in this monograph, I need not try to explain its theme or the method he has adopted to work it out. Before he took it up as his project during the tenure of his Fellowship at this Institute we had a long discussion on both, and I felt convinced that here was a good scope indeed for a worthwhile piece of experimental study, one which was likely to give to all students of Indian archaeology, history and anthropology an insight into the nature of their respective disciplines and what they could yield if and when an integrated approach could be made. While on his work Dr. Malik was kind enough to keep me in close touch; he also gave me the benefit of reading through the chapters as they were taking shape and form and of discussing many a point in the process, for which I feel very thankful to him.

The monograph is frankly an experimental study in methodology of research, analysis and interpretation in the field of archaeology, history and anthropology, and should be treated as such, to my mind. Whether the findings of Dr. Malik will endure or not, is for experts in the field to try out and decide. Meanwhile I feel happy that the Indian Institute of Advanced Study could extend to him an opportunity to carry out a project that was uppermost in his mind, and place the results of his study in the hands of experts in the relevant fields in the form of a monograph, and this in the shortest possible time. I hope they will find it worth their while to read it through and give some serious thought to its theme, which it certainly deserves.

Simla   NIHARRANJAN RAY
October 30, 1968.

CONTENTS

LIST OF FIGURES AND MAPS

ACKNOWLEDGEMENTS

In the writing of this monograph it is not possible to restrict my gratefulness to those who were of 'immediate' help. I cannot help thinking of those who have been sources of inspiration in moulding my thoughts and ideas about archaeology in India. Foremost among these were Professors Childe and Zeuner during my post-graduate studies at the University of London, and later on, Professor Subbarao at the M.S. University of Baroda. More recently, however, I have been greatly influenced by the ideas and orientation of the members of the Department of Anthropology, University of Chicago (U.S.A.), specially Professors Braidwood, Milton Singer, Robert M. Adams and Lewis R. Binford (now at the University of California, Los Angeles). I am grateful to all of them for widening my horizons in both archaeology and anthropology.

But it would not have been possible to complete a monograph such as this through mere inspiration. It was equally important for me to be given the requisite facilities and opportunities to sit down and write this monograph. These were provided to me by, first, the authorities of the M.S. University of Baroda who very graciously permitted me study-leave soon after my return from Chicago and, secondly, by Professor Niharranjan Ray, Director, Indian Institute of Advanced Study. Professor Ray has not only helped me in writing this monograph through various discussions but also by allowing me complete freedom to pursue this task. It is this freedom to not only speculate and 'experiment' with newer ideas but also the freedom from many non-academic duties which, to my mind, is very crucial if higher research, specially in humanities and social sciences, has to come of age in India. These fundamental requisites are hard to find in India. I am grateful to Professor Ray for all this, and to the other members of the administrative staff of this Institute who have helped me in different ways to complete the monograph, specially Shri R. K. Sethi, the Publication Officer.

My thanks are also due to Shri Khatri and Shri Panchal, draughtsmen of the Department of Archaeology, M.S. University of Baroda, for figs. 3 to 10. It was very kind of my brother, Keshev Malik, to go through the final draft. Finally, I am grateful to Zarine, my wife, not only for the help rendered through the various stages of the monograph but also in many other ways.

20 May 1968
Simla

S. C. MALIK

INTRODUCTION

In recent years the basic interests of the sciences dealing with the 'human phenomenon' have been in the direction of explanation rather than mere description. By adopting certain conceptual schemes such interdisciplinary attacks on problems of common interest have been variously referred to as the 'multi-dimensional', 'problem-oriented' or the 'structural-functional' approach, depending upon the particular humanistic science that is included in the scheme. In Anthropology this inter-disciplinary approach emerged during the recent wars as a result of the need for highly integrated information covering a large number of relevant variables. It was realized that cultural data alone was not sufficient, any more than the sociological, psychological, political or economic to answer the needs for information required for the prediction that accompanied highly organized psychological, economic, political and military warfare. "It depended not on the contribution of Anthropology itself but on the affiliation of anthropologists with members of other disciplines, where team work was the rule".[1] But this integrative approach was not in vogue when I was a student of Anthropology at college. Archaeology was then, as even now it is, a subdiscipline of Anthropology, just as it was, and is also, a part of the curricula of Ancient History in Indian universities. However, both Anthropology and History tended to treat, as is the case today, their various subdisciplines as separate units even though in theory their study implied the total study of Man and Society. The traditional concept of both the intra- and interdisciplinary effort amounted, as it seems to continue even now in many of our universities, to a simple federation or co-existence of the classificatory groups of data relating to Man.

Integration then simply meant the combination of data, that is, research was collaborative rather than organized along any definitive common conceptual schemes. Therefore, History and Anthropology in India have not become integrative disciplines in the full sense of the term and the teaching of these subjects follows a similar pattern.

However, it did not worry me, then, whether our major discipline was an integrated one or a federal one since some of us were later, at the post-graduate level, too involved in learning the rigours of one or the other subdisciplines. I was specializing in prehistoric archaeology and found that carrying out explorations, excavations, and writing reports was very exciting. All this continues to be just as fascinating. But, as a decade went by, I also found that this general archaeological routine was somewhat 'dull', in a sense. I specially felt this when I was thinking about the interpretation and the organization of the recovered archaeological evidence in terms of the 'total' study of Man and Society. I wondered what all these technical advances such as scientific techniques, total excavations, new typologies, field surveys, distribution maps, etc. added upto, apart from knowing an enormous complicated body of 'facts'. All this hard work and sweat did not directly and meaningfully correlate to any understanding of human society, specially to its contemporary situation. Apart from all this, the intellectual 'flavour' which was present in many of the other social and humanistic sciences was missing in the study of this history-oriented Indian archaeology. At any rate, in thus 'rethinking archaeology', my interest in general anthropology was revived and I began to re-evaluate the history of archaeological studies in India, along with some of the more recent works.

It is on reading the various reports that one realizes the scant attention that has been devoted in them to the theoretical aspects of archaeology. Here, theory means not only the formulation of certain models, frames of reference but also the critical

examination of words, concepts and terminologies which archaeologists want to use or even already employ. This meaning
of theory does not include the importance that is given to discussions on chronological problems, methods of horizontal or
vertical excavations, etc., or even the casual hypotheses that
are formulated at the end of an archaeological report. By and
large, all these current discussions and interpretations of archaeological data have been — and are — carried out mainly on the
descriptive level. This indicates a sad lack of not only an
integrative approach but also of any sound theoretical base.
Nevertheless, many archaeologists will claim that archaeology
in India has now both a theoretical as well as an integrative
interdisciplinary approach because of its use of ethnographic
and physical anthropological data and techniques, and by its
adoption of the methodology of the techniques of the natural
and physical sciences. But this dependence on a multitude of
sciences amounts to mere collaboration rather than 'true' integration. However, an explanation of the absence of a regular
body theory or the current disdain for the use of any integrative
(social science) approach with regard to archaeological phenomena may be found in a critical examination of the history of
archaeological studies in India. It shows that archaeology in
India has in fact evolved without any specific sophisticated theoretical foundations, and most of its workers have mainly been
influenced by such disciplines as history, geology, art and architecture, along with their respective concepts and objectives in
the recovery of archaeological remains. The past one hundred
years, at least, of archaeological research have produced little
interpretative results in terms of any social science approach
(such as the processual concepts of 'how' and 'why') because
relatively few professional archaeologists in India have come
into it by way of anthropology. Therefore, it is no surprise to
note that the current interpretations continue to employ the
traditional descriptive concepts of 'when' and 'where'. But,

to my mind, the continuation of this approach places the final goal of archaeology to dig up 'people', 'humanity', etc. to be rather distant.

Archaeological studies have, therefore, now reached a stage in India when some searching questions have to be asked with regard to the basic premises of its research, in order to be generated by basic innovations in ideas. In doing this it becomes a necessary first step to reject any 'reified' or one-sided traditional explanations of archaeological phenomena before any new means and schemes of the social sciences are adopted. It is by the adoption of a social science approach which will enable us to give a fuller interpretation of the social and cultural aspects of archaeological remains. It is only thus that archaeology will be able to contribute to the growth of the social and humanistic sciences, and it may even venture out and carry on research projects by developing a philosophy of its own. In this way archaeology may eventually become a vigorous theoretic and intellectual discipline, and its facts and interpretations will also become of increasing relevance both to the contemporary scene and to our philosophical outlook. This last concern with some kind of philosophies, to my mind, is a very essential task of archaeology and, therefore, requires a fuller explanation because it forms the background of the theme of this monograph. It is on the basis of this background that there is also a justification for one to suggest a reorientation of the goals of archaeology in India, which is as given below.

II

What is archaeological knowledge ? A simple short answer would be that archaeological knowledge is an attempt by the archaeologist to reconstruct the 'past-as-it-was', or historical reality. But the problem and its answer in fact lie within the much wider general realm of the epistemology of the study of the past. However, without going into the wider problem we shall very briefly discuss this with specific reference to archaeology. The approach to the problem of the past, as has been dealt with by students of philosophy,[2] is governed by our perceptual, conceptual and metaphysical reproductions of the external world. An examination of the metaphysical aspects of this problem is not possible in this context since these exist independently of any proofs. Let us, therefore, take up the other two very briefly.

The perceptual reproductions of the external world include both the illusions and delusions that affect the sense data and on which is based an ideal reproduction of the world. But included in these reproductions of the 'external' perceptual 'reality', archaeological phenomena in our case, are also any private errors and mistakes due to sense-perceptions which are as such accepted by society to become knowledge. This knowledge is also often distorted by certain of our unconscious value-judgements which are inevitable, and have a considerable effect in the research of archaeology at all levels. Therefore, all that is possible for the individual archaeologist to do, in order consciously to avoid distortions due to sense-perception and value-judgements, etc., is to increase his physical and mental awareness, specially the qualities of objectivity, empathy, curiosity and tolerance for ambiguity, uncertainty and the indeterminate. But this manner of thinking involves a 'way of life' which is governed not only by the rigours of science but also by many other attitudes. However, this interesting problem is beyond the scope of the present discussion since it is concerned with the direct and indirect socio-cultural 'educational' influences that play upon the performance of the individual archaeologist.

The conceptual reproductions of the external world, on the other hand, are subtle and persistent and greatly affect archaeological research, despite the statements of many archaeologists

who would like to consider it as a mere descriptive discipline because it has so far been minus conscious concepts and
hypotheses. For instance, the evolutionary approach to current
archaeological problems is the significant outcome of the evolutionary concepts of 18th century Europe, to which Darwin's
Theory of Evolution had given considerable impetus. Similarly,
today, it is probably because of the 'materialistic' conceptual
reproductions of our age which set at a premium technological
innovation and economic development, that archaeology gives
so much importance to the techno-economic aspects of archaeological societies even though we have nothing by which to assume that prehistoric man cared more for durable remains than
susceptible decaying materials. Again, in India, many of us
continue to follow the 19th century diffusionist concepts of the
old German schools of anthropology and of the British school
that was headed by G. Eliot Smith and W. J. Perry. Both these
schools had based their assumptions on certain *a priori* grounds
which took for granted an extreme degree of conservatism of
human society. Fundamental to their approach was the hypothesis that a given cultural element, or a complex of traits, can
retain its identity while being passed on from one people to
another over the principal parts of the earth's inhabited surfaces.
It is the influence of this school that has effected the interpretation of certain archaeological phenomena in India. To give
one example, there is the commonmost interpretation of the
Harappan evidence which is described as a 'static' and conservative society. In short, all description is related, in one way
or another, to concepts and the conceptual reproductions of
the external world.

Thus, every 'society' interprets the past according to its
contemporary thought and philosophy, i.e., according to that
society's perceptual, conceptual and metaphysical reproductions
of·the external world. Hence, the historical reality of each
society, diverges from every other spatially or temporally related

society. Therefore, any reconstructions or reproductions of past
societies are 'true' in only as far as they enjoy social (whether
it is a group of archaeologists, historians, etc., or society
at large) endorsement. But this historical 'reality' becomes
false as and when new perceptual and conceptual divergences
make the older reproductions 'out of date', that is, not only
because of the new evidences of a factual perceptual kind which
are discovered but also because of the formulation of new conceptual schemes. Therefore, in this sense, both the meaning
of statements with regard to the past and the range of evidence
are 'unstable'. But this does not mean that there is no 'truth'
or 'falsehood' about any statements with regard to the past
because, at any given moment, if all the available evidence de-
monstrates that a certain event in all probability had occurred,
then there is no reason to suppose that this event did not in fact
occur. But again, this does not mean, certainly, that the event
had in fact occurred as formally entailed by the evidence. The
possibility that the evidence is deceptive must remain open;
and this is not only in the sense that further evidence may fail
to corroborate it. It must at least be conceivable that the event
did not in fact occur at all, even though from time to time when
the question is raised all the evidence that will be ever forth-
coming goes to show that it did. For example, the event of
the large-scale massacre of the Harappans, in the late levels,
was once considered an historical reality. But, now, according
to the latest findings, this event had most probably never
taken place because the earlier interpretation was the result
of an erroneous reading of the stratigraphic evidence. Therefore, the question that now arises is: Is it ever possible
to reconstruct the 'past-as-it-was' and how is one to
verify the 'truth' and 'falsehood' about the statements of
archaeology ?

The problem of the verifiability of archaeological statements
in terms of historical reality is not unique to it since one equally

faces the verifiability of a statement whether it refers to the past, present or future. Archaeological statements with or without chronological content are only statements with a factual content and are referred to as statements of the past because they indicate the temporal relationship of the research worker to them, describing an event which is earlier than the occasion of it being expressed. But this means that one is still confronted with the problem of showing how one can be justified in accepting statements which purport to describe past events. It seems that if one is justified at all, it is by means of the inductive argument. The conclusion as such is not verifiable. But, still, in any inductive argument one statement about the past is used to justify another; there are no independent means of justifying them all. The possibilities of recapturing the 'past-as-it-was' are impossible because one occupies a particular position in time at any given moment and hence, difficulties of a temporal nature prevent one from observing the actual event. Therefore, if the past 'reality' is accessible at all, it is only because of one's imagination that can roam about freely, and is acceptable only if tempered by the currently valid and verifiable statements of both general and particular knowledge. In archaeology it is, of course, by means of empirical knowledge that one can observe the past, that is, this is in the form of some surviving objects from the past that represent the embodiments of human thoughts and ideas. But by archaeological means one certainly cannot observe the events themselves and, therefore, the observed phenomena of archaeology are the only reason for one to believe that the past events did occur. But in the absence of performing physical feats of temporal projection, our belief has to be based on certain canons of knowledge of the humanistic and the social sciences which enable one to at least theoretically observe past events. These canons of knowledge, however, are not (and should not be) static since it is not only the theoretical framework of interpretation but also of

the method of observation of past phenomena that continuously changes with the passage of time. Therefore, we might
say that there are only degrees of archaeological truth and
historical reality is unattainable in any absolute sense of its
independent existence, and is relative.

This brief discussion is a crucial one for us because it emphasises the fact that archaeology is, in this sense, chiefly
a theoretical quest for a knowledge of the past and is, therefore,
closer to philosophy—scientific philosophy. Thus, if the progress
of Indian archaeology is viewed in this light, we see that it has
stayed at a static 'intellectual' level because it continues to use
19th century concepts, by a steady accumulation of data, and
is too involved with chronology and taxonomic schemes. But
even scientific ideas and concepts are not immune to the
influence of fashion and it is high time that Indian archaeology outgrew its old historiography and evolutionistic schools
of thought which to a great extent are implicit in the data
of archaeology. It must, therefore, encompass new ideas, such
as a social science method of analysis, and develop its own
concepts and techniques, its own tacit fundamental way of
seeing archaeological phenomena. In this manner, as archaeological knowledge advances and its techniques improve, the
framework of personal ideas in which each student of the subject will try to concentrate and express what he learns will alter
the shape of archaeology. What is being implied here is that
such an archaeologist will in fact have to be a kind of 'philosopher' because it will be necessary for him to not only critically
examine the various concepts, terms, etc. of the historical
and anthropological disciplines that he does consciously
or unconsciously borrow, but also the ideas and concepts of
many other seemingly remote disciplines. It is only thus that
archaeology will be able to relate itself to the present growth
and understanding of life and to the nature of reality
itself.

III

At this point, in order to further justify the reasons for a re-assessment of the aims and methods of archaeological studies, let us now come down from the somewhat abstract level to a more concrete level, i.e., the relevance of a social science approach for Indian archaeology. The social science framework for archaeological and historical data is very crucial in a case like India because here the past lives so obviously and strongly. Therefore, because of this long continuity, it becomes one of the most important and imperative tasks of archaeology to relate its data to the present, and thereby provide a long-range meaningful understanding of some of the problems of contemporary Indian society and its situation. But this is only possible by means of a social science orientation, and archaeology will also by this means become of sound 'practical' utility. However, there should normally be no grounds, in terms of 'usefulness', by which one should justify, either in theory or in practice, one's desire for an advance in any learning or to increase precision of knowledge in any given discipline. But, then, there are some important reasons for such a 'utilitarian' viewpoint which by itself, apart from the 'philosophical' viewpoint stated in the previous section, warrants a justification for the re-evaluation of archaeological aims and methods in India. But this 'utilitarian' viewpoint does not mean the normally well-understood 'use' of the past, which we know is to increase the simple general awareness of the time perspective of human history. The 'practical' justification for the social science approach to the study of archaeology may be stated as follows.

Every day, men, both lay and academic, very often justify their statements and arguments which are made at public and private occasions by quoting from India's remote and very recent past. For example, in 1818, Ram Mohan Roy published his tract against *sati*, which was supported by his study of the

Śāstras. In the fifties of the same century, Ishwarchandra Vidyasagar supported his arguments for widow remarriage by referring to the *Smṛiti* literature, as also did the social reformer, Swami Dayanand, in the seventies of the 19th century. On the other hand, B. G. Tilak cited the same Sanskrit texts against the age of Consent Bill[3] in order to establish that a girl should be married before she had attained maturity. But what is more commonly noticed is that such statements about the past are often erroneous because these are generally based on secondary and tertiary sources. This may be largely because laymen have to depend upon research literature which is often abstruse and incomplete. Moreover, scholars of past studies have seldom cared to make any sound and simple generalizing statements, specially those which will help us to understand some problems of the present. However, there is no question about the relevance of history proper in understanding contemporary problems, and in this attempts have been made to use the past both by the academic and by the lay. But many readers would question at once both the immediate psychic relevance as well as any other 'use' of prehistoric archaeology, specially for the understanding of any of our contemporary problems. Prehistory is commonly regarded, if not often, as something very remote and mysterious and which, at the most, may be considered useful for mere chronicling purposes.

It is, indeed, difficult to provide proof of the direct utility of archaeology to the present and even harder for prehistory to indicate its pertinence in framing and executing policies for the conduct of affairs, either public or private. Nevertheless, statements, specially the political ones, in India are full of references even to the remote past whenever the need arises to impress the validity of these statements, or rather the dogmas and assertions. As is well known, there are numerous examples of this frequent recourse to ancient historical and archaeological knowledge by social reformists and political leaders. But Indian archaeologists (historians), in spite of knowing about the obvious — though erroneous — social use of their field of study, have not made any general attempts to widen the theoretical horizons of their discipline, if only in order to enable one to give broader interpretations which one could then relate to certain important problems of the contemporary situation.

However, it is not only the lay who attempt to support their respective statements or hypotheses by the use of different constructs of the 'past-as-it-was', but knowledge of the past is also often made use of by the members of such academic disciplines as economics, art history, sociology, political science, etc. By and large, once again, the use is from secondary and tertiary sources. Admittedly, it is not expected from members of these disciplines, in this age of specialization when the tremendous increase of factual knowledge is difficult to keep pace with, to check the source material for either archaeological or historical evidence. But the fact remains that colleagues from the other humanistic and social sciences do constantly reinforce their own concepts from some sort of imprecise and incomplete generalizations that they are able to find at the end of an historical or archaeological study. On the other hand, Indian historians and archaeologists, even more often, employ a lay commonsense knowledge of such important relevant concepts as Man, Society, Nature, etc., that is, they employ these words and concepts without ever caring to define them in terms of the current usage in the social and behavioural sciences. The result is, to turn full circle, that the conclusions which are arrived at by the archaeologist (historian) get incorporated as a feed-back into the other social and humanistic sciences and further on to the lay public. Thus, for instance, in this century one of the indirect causes of the world wars may have been the spread of faulty knowledge of the past of other nations and peoples, or such other erroneous notions as 'primitive' versus 'civilized', 'inferior' versus 'superior' races, etc. These notions were derived from the early descriptive 'colonial' research phase of the study of anthropology, and this knowledge then most probably incorporated itself into the popular and political thought which ultimately led the civilized world into these dehumanizing wars, the end of which seems no nearer.

In any case, it is on grounds of such briefly stated 'practical' importance, apart from the justification of advancing learning for its own sake, that there is ample justification for a re-evaluation of the fundamental concepts of archaeological research so that it can also develop a philosophy of its own and be of some constructive "social use". But "pursued for its own sake... (it)... is only to be found as a profession among others by which man earns his living, and as such is worth little because it has removed from its source whence it arose and in which it can renew itself".[4] But by this social use it is not meant that there should be a campaign for the mass popularization of archaeology by lay exhibitions, radio and television talks, etc. These programmes usually glorify India, or one of its regions, either on emotional grounds through its 'oldness' or through the aesthetic appeal of its art treasures, etc. These programmes are only of 'use' in a limited way.

IV

To conclude and summarize, the foregoing thoughts were uppermost in my mind when I decided to attempt this monograph, steering away from the main path of archaeological studies in India. The only manner, at this first stage, by which I could fulfil my obligation to the profession of archaeology was by clarifying certain thoughts with regard to the broad concepts, and to show that the results of archaeological research are of great relevance to the present. Therefore, the object of this monograph is not to make any novel contribution to the archaeology of India in the sense of presenting any new excavation results, etc. *The simple aim is to stimulate interest in the development of different approaches to the study of archaeology rather than to present any definitive results.* I hope that in this manner certain new research guidelines will enable us to extract such socio-cultural information about past societies which at present is either lacking or at best is lamentably defective. The data of Indian archaeology, today, which have been accumulated over the last hundred years or more, are over-shadowed by traditional research guidelines to such an extent that even many of the contemporary elemental theoretical currents of the social and behavioural sciences are not utilized. In fact, Indian archaeology does not have a theoretical base in the sense of a body of theory which a physicist or an anthropologist would recognize as such albeit there cannot be a general theory for archaeology as there is in the physical sciences. But the unsystematic use of the various frames of reference today, in India, seem to be incapable of providing a wholly convincing picture of archaeology on its own. It is, therefore, imperative, as is increasingly the case outside India, that Indian archaeology should seek the help of such social sciences as anthropology and sociology because archaeology is now taken up to mean the "whole anthropology of extinct cultures". "The breadth of this spectrum must properly equate with the essential nature of man. . . from the biological to the cultural end. . . . (they). . . must concern themselves with the total cultures of the extinct peoples they excavate and have no right of preemption. . . I believe that we archaeologists sell our potential contribution to knowledge short when we think of our field as strictly subdivided".[5]

The time is now ripe for the sophistication of our discipline since, compared to the other social and humanistic sciences, it is far below the highest conceivable intellectual level and, therefore, at a 'naive' theoretical stage. Moreover, in the light of the present world of 'crisis' in which man is striving to 'find' himself in this transition towards a New Age, a sure understanding of the old assumes even greater significance. Consequently, the facts of archaeology, both the historic and prehistoric, are far from being either irrelevant or 'dead'. Both from the academic as well as from the practical point of view, a thorough and precise reconstruction of archaeological (historical) evidence, and from it an overall understanding of past societal and cultural processes is therefore a very fundamental one. But the solution to overcome any conceptual misinterpretations and misunderstandings, or the application of the integrative interdisciplinary approach, involves the employment of effective intellectual operations for archaeology. I am not, however, suggesting that in the past the archaeologist (historian) has been any less intelligent and effective in producing true and workable statements. It would, perhaps, be equally idle to dwell upon the intellectual merits and demerits of past performances because "concerning what archaeology is . . . seems to me to be what archaeologists do. . . . There is probably no other profession so vulnerable to poseur and charlatan. But were I to excommunicate here and now all non-professionals, I should have little left of the history of archaeology".[6] However, it is essential to at least carry out some very brief critical appraisals of a few of the important works of Indian archaeology, specially in order to learn from past experience. This is the only manner by which one may hope to illustrate the nature of archaeological interpretations that were present in the past and, thereby, know the consciously or unconsciously accepted concepts which archaeologists had adopted, and have continued to follow in their work today. This appraisal follows in the next chapter.

At the first stage of writing this monograph, in the absence of verification in the field (which will be the second stage for the present approach here), it was only possible to exemplify this viewpoint by applying certain concepts and propositions from anthropology to the archaeological evidence that was already available in the reports. Moreover, I have attempted this despite the drawback of basing my hypothesis on meagre evidence concerning many periods of India's culture-history that was available in the reports. But this meagre evidence need not worry us since this monograph is about the questions raised in order to look at archaeological evidence in India in a different way. One of the basic assumptions here is that advances in any given field of knowledge are made by devising newer hypotheses for further appraisal, exploration, testing, correction and generalization. Therefore, in due course, the frames of reference given in this monograph may have to be altered either because of new evidences that are produced or because of better models (frames of reference) which will be formulated than those which I have borrowed and suggested. The usefulness of this monograph will, I hope, be in suggesting some new trends and giving an impetus and aid to future archaeological research, writing and teaching. I firmly believe that Indian archaeology needs the infusion of new ideas and trends in its method and theory, in order to lead to a fuller understanding of not only the specific problems of Indian archaeology but also of the problems of Indian society, culture and civilization in general. In this context, one of the important last suggestions of the late Professor Gordon Childe was along these lines:

"The economic, sociological and ultimately historical interpretations of archaeological data has, I believe, now become a main task that can contribute enormously to human history and should enhance the status of archaeology. . . . No prehistorian can be content with describing, however functionally, his culture as a finished static organism. It must not only function, it must change and the observed changes must be described and explained. In doing so it is all too easy to appeal to external factors, to influences from foreign culture and even migrations. A prehistorian would be well advised to employ a version of

Occam's razor and invoke external factors only when compelled by cogent concrete evidence... A prehistorian, like any other historian, should not only be content to describe, but also to explain, historical description should be at the same time explanatory. Phenomena should be so described that they are seen as instances of general familiar principles ... the future of archaeology lies, I believe, with the historical rather than the naturalistic disciplines. It is a source of history... No doubt the archaeologist is pre-disposed towards materialism... He cannot, however, logically be a complete materialist: for bits of dead matter become even archaeologist's data in so far as they are expressions and symbols of human thought and volition, of ideas and purposes that transcend not only each particular embodiment in archaeological datum, but also each individual actor or thinker being social and is therefore immaterial!"[7]

NOTES AND REFERENCES

1. Bennet, John W., " Interdisciplinary Research and the Concept of Culture ", *American Anthropologist*, 56, 1954, pp. 169-179.
2. Ayer, A. J., *The Problem of Knowledge*, Penguin, 1956.
3. Sharma, R. S., *Light on Early Indian Society and Economy*, Manaktalas, Bombay, 1966, pp. 2-3.
4. Croce, Benedetto, *History as the Story of Liberty*, London, 1941, pp. 138-139.
5. Braidwood, R. J., " Archaeology and the Evolutionary Theory ", *Evolution: A Centennial Appraisal*, ed. Betty J. Meggars, Anthropological Society of Washington, Washington D.C., 1959, p. 79.
6. Ibid., p. 77.
7. Childe, V. G., " Valediction ", *Bulletin of the Institute of Archaeology*, I, London, 1958, pp. 1-8.

THE BACKGROUND

A HISTORICAL SKETCH

The history of archaeological and ancient historical studies in India may be divided into four periods. The first begins with Sir William Jones in the 18th century, from 1784 until 1861. The second from 1861 until 1902 with Cunningham who was given charge of the Archaeological Survey of India in 1861. The third from 1902 until 1944, with the appointment of the far-sighted Lord Curzon. The fourth is the recent one from 1944 onwards, when Sir Mortimer Wheeler became the Director-General of the Survey. Elaborate accounts of this history are available elsewhere,[1] from where this part of the chapter has been condensed. The chief objective here is only to give a background in order to bring out the salient features and the controlling assumptions that in the past have governed archaeological work in India. A major portion of the history of Indian archaeology is about the work that was carried out by the departments of the Government of India.

Period I (1784-1861)

It begins with Sir William Jones who started the Asiatic Society in Calcutta with the aim of enquiring "into the History, the Antiquities, Arts and Sciences and Literatures of Asia".[2] There were others before Jones who had been interested in the antiquities of India, but these were dilettante activities. Similar societies were formed in Bombay and Madras soon after, but one cannot say that this pioneering research was truly of an archaeological nature. These studies had really emerged on the basis of literary research with little knowledge of the archaeological technique of excavations and were mainly confined

18

to translations or to "highly speculative dissertations",[3] in the belief that "the function of the monuments was only to elucidate the scattered information which can yet be collected from the remains of Indian literature".[4] The range of interests these pioneers had was very wide, from ethnology to mathematics, geology, meteorology, etc., and as expected, the conclusions arrived at were of such a wide general nature that these would be considered absurd by us today.

Nevertheless, this was to be the groundwork for further research and progress in the field, such as the accurate observation and recording of monuments in the field. It took place in 1800, when the Government of India appointed Francis Buchanan to survey Mysore. He was "the first to realize the value of detailed plans and exact measurements of ancient buildings and historic sites".[5] Further impetus to this approach was not officially given until the arrival of James Princep in 1833, who with his scientifically trained background unlocked the mystery of the Brahmi and Kharoshthi scripts and showed equal clear-sightedness in emphasising the value of accurate field survey and precise recordings.[6] However, it seems that the objectives of obtaining the plans of old buildings, new art treasures, coins and epigraphic records, was largely to enrich the museums.

Thus, until 1861, with increasing interest taken by the Government of India, architectural surveys and recording continued along with the aims "of drawings of objects of interest. . . illustrative of the . . . phases, characters and conditions of its various . . . peoples comprising architecture, implements, costumes, etc.".[7] In short, the first period was dominated by what may be called antiquarian research.

Period II (1861-1902)

In the year 1848, Alexander Cunningham had submitted a plan to the Governor-General, Lord Canning, to establish an Archaeological Survey of India, and its aims were defined as, "an accurate description illustrated by plans, measurements, drawings or photographs and by copies of inscriptions of such remains as deserve notice, with the histories of them so far as it may be traceable, and records of the traditions that are retained regarding them".[8]   This plan materialized in 1861 with Cunningham as the man-in-charge, and in 1863 an Act was passed whereby the monuments could be preserved and protected. Until 1865, Cunningham had carried out a great deal of work along topographical lines.   But during his absence from 1865 to 1870, the Survey was abolished and attention was paid to the photographing of monuments and preparation of casts of architectural pieces.[9]   However, on his return in 1870, the Survey was re-established under his Director-Generalship to carry out a good job of survey and exploration specially in the North and North-East India.   But while the world of archaeology "was in a state of ferment",[10] because of the work and discoveries of Schliemann in Hissarlik in 1871, Cunningham continued to be dominated by antiquarian research aims of "discovering monuments and remains, revisiting old ones and bringing to light coins, inscriptions, sculptures and other antiquities".[11]   It was because of this that he remained indifferent to the work that was being carried out since the 1880's by Bruce Foote and his colleagues in prehistory.   No wonder, he even overlooked identifying the Harappan civilization when he simply dismissed a Harappan pictographic seal and a sherd which were shown to him.   Cunningham, however, initiated good work in Indian epigraphy which was later put on a sound footing in 1872 by James Burgess who was an architect by training.

On Cunningham's retirement, James Burgess became the Director-General in 1885, for a period of three years.   He set forth his aims as, "Archaeology being but the history of art. . . (it has) to provide a pretty full illustration and history of ancient and medieval architecture down to the decline of the Muhammaden style".[12]   The retirement of Burgess led once more to the abolition of the Survey and to a chaotic state until 1902.

During the second period, important developments were **also** taking place in the field of Indian prehistory. In 1863, the **year** Lyell published the geological evidence for the antiquity of Man, Bruce Foote discovered the first palaeolith near Madras and earlier, in 1860, Le Mesurier discovered a 'neolith'. But this progress of prehistoric studies was interrelated with research in geology and its concepts and, therefore, its work was mainly carried out by the Geological Survey of India to which Foote belonged. The aims of prehistoric research in India were much the same as in Europe, that is, to locate fossil man and his remains so as to push back the date of the existence of Early Man. Similarly, artifacts were mostly described as 'bouchers' following the archtype known in France at that time, and the handaxes from South India were described and classified as pre-chellean, rostrocarinates, etc. Thus, flakes which did not form a part of the European palaeolithic assemblages were also overlooked in the Indian context since they did not conform to definitive known attractive types. (This trend and inheritance of copying European classificatory and conceptual systems has not left many Indian prehistorians even today, who like to interpret the Indian 'Stone Age' evidence on the basis of prevailing European nomenclature without properly understanding not only the cultural but also the geological implications of this borrowing.) In any case, Foote carried out pioneering research because he had built up a vast index collection of prehistoric antiquities which he primarily arranged in a relative chronological order. This techno-typological approach to prehistory continued until 1930.

Period III (1902-1944)

The post of the Director-General of the Archaeological Survey of India was re-established in 1902 by Lord Curzon, whose conception of archaeology was much more comprehensive than had previously been the case, because it included exploration, excavation, research, epigraphy, publication, preservation of monuments and the establishment of museums. Earlier in 1900, in a speech to the Asiatic Society of Bengal, Lord Curzon had clearly said: "Epigraphy should not be set behind research any more than research should be set behind conservation. All are ordered parts of any scientific scheme of antiquarian work . . . It is, in my judgement, equally our duty to dig and to discover, to classify, reproduce and describe, to copy and decipher, and to cherish and conserve."[13] Nevertheless, he had to fight against heavy odds of the long established tradition of inherited prejudice in order to establish the Survey on a sound and secure foundation.

In 1902, Lord Curzon assigned this formidable task to John Marshall who became the Director-General at the age of only twenty-six. Marshall "realized that the prime need at that time was conservation and excavation, and he deprecated the spending of undue time by the archaeological officers on literary research".[14] It was most probably the inheritance of this approach which later on resulted in studies being carried on in isolation both by the historian and the archaeologist. However, Marshall's excavation activities were mainly confined to the period of history proper, specially the Buddhist sites, in continuation of the tradition set by Cunningham. But there were, of course, notable exceptions such as Marshall's excavation of the non-Buddhist sites at Bhita, Pāṭalīputra, Taxila, and the Indus Valley sites. Nevertheless, Buddhist sites were given prominence because more was known of them through the accounts of the Chinese pilgrims and earlier researches. It was also because of the spectacular nature of the finds at the Buddhist sites which made it easier to get public and financial support. However, there seems to be a general opinion that the main tendency of Marshall was more to assure public interest than for the sake of the specialized professional archaeologist. It is for this reason that he seems to have conducted large-scale excavations at Mohenjodaro, Taxila, Sarnath and Nālandā that yielded a large number of excavated objects. It is also because of this over-emphasis on 'antiquities' that, later on, Marshall and his associates have been criticized for the inadequate excavation techniques that were employed. He has been criticized for ignoring the principle of stratified excavations prevalent in Europe at that time, and also for not carrying out excavations that should have been spread out all over the subcontinent in order to obtain the regional culture-indices.

Marshall retired in 1928, and the Director-Generals who succeeded him carried on the work with more or less similar aims and objectives, even though there were many changes in the administrative and financial policies of the Survey. In 1932, the change in the Ancient Monuments and Preservations Act led to the participation of American Institutions such as the American School of Indian and Iranian Studies, the Boston Museum of Fine Arts, and the Yale and Cambridge Universities' geological-cum-prehistoric expedition. But in spite of all this increased activity, in 1939 the Survey came under the heavy but hurried (and yet partly justified) criticism of Sir Leonard Wooley who was specially called to India to prepare a report. His opinion was asked because "the fact was that Indian archaeologists had not kept in touch with the techniques of excavation improved in Europe and America, with the result that the methods followed by them were antiquated. Hardly any attempt had been made to establish sequences of cultures by deep excavations, and there was no systematic plan about the choice of sites to be excavated, so that the archaeology of large parts of the country had remained in the dark".[15] On Wooley's recommendation large-scale excavations were undertaken "at Ahichchhatrā during the years 1940-44 under the direction of Dikshit. Particular attention was paid to the classification of historical pottery-types, ranging over about fifteen centuries, which had been practically ignored before" [16]

Dikshit also organized the Indian "prehistoric party", to explore the Sabarmati Valley of Gujarat, and he revived the lost personal contacts with provincial museums and departments of archaeology of various Indian States. "Encouraged by him, the University of Calcutta took a license for excavating the ancient site of Bangarh, District Dinajpur, Bengal, and thus marked itself out as the first Indian University to take an interest in excavation". [17]

Period IV (1944 onwards)

The appointment of Wheeler in 1944 brought about significant even if not radically different changes because he introduced into India the rigorous observation of stratified excavation to bring it into line with the best of international standards. To further this aim, he organized training camps for excavations, explorations and conservation courses. These helpful courses were meant both for the Survey staff as well as research workers from the universities and other institutions. Each of Wheeler's "excavations achieved the specific purpose for which it had been undertaken. He aimed at establishing some firm datum lines in Indian Archaeology to which all results accruing out of future excavations could be correlated". [18]

Thus, today, the inheritance from Wheeler's leadership during the last decades is that of the application of modern methods of archaeology for the scientific recovery of material remains, in terms of the concepts of 'when' and 'where'. Similarly, the work that was carried out in prehistory by Burkitt and his colleagues in the 1930's, and from 1949 onwards by the late Prof. F. E. Zeuner, was also aimed at establishing a sound chronological framework for Peninsular India. This pioneering work in prehistory of laying a firm foundation for the chronology of the subcontinent of India was very necessary for further archaeological work.

Such in brief is the historical background of the Indian historic and prehistoric archaeological studies. It was necessary to sketch this in order that one may be able to discern the inheritance of the later aims and concepts during the last decade or so. The question that now arises is, have our aims and methods changed and is there any new 'direction' for the progress of Indian archaeology ? The answers to this will be examined below by a brief critical appraisal of some of the well-known 'recent' works in Indian prehistory in terms of the explicit or implicit concepts underlying them.

II

(1) *Progress in Prehistory*[19] may be taken up as one of the early (1953) comprehensive essays on the prehistory of India because it is indicative of the guidelines which were set forth for the next decade's work. The framework of the prehistoric sequence suggested in this essay was that of Christian Thomson's threefold division of the history of mankind into the Ages of Stone, Bronze and Iron along with their finer subdivisions. Therefore, the main concern here seems to have been with typology and with the establishment of a chronology. The Indian succession was viewed in the light of the then known European one, and this appears to have been the chief concern in discussing the various problems. But it is also worthwhile to note the terms and concepts which seem to underlie some of the statements made in this essay, such as: "The stone industries *succeeding* the Lower Palaeolithic in north and south India pose very interesting problems. As in other parts of the Old World is there an independent Upper Palaeolithic blade-and-burin industry in India ? Microlithic industries are fairly widespread all over India. Sometimes microliths are found in association

with pottery, neoliths and copper tools. Lastly, though neo-lithic artifacts are so widespread, *we still do not know how they came into India*"[20] (Italics mine). In analysing this statement, it may be noticed that the use of some of the words such as 'succeeding' is the result of, first, a borrowing of the concept of 'succession' from the discipline of geology. Secondly, its ori-ginal context has been overlooked and in using it in the context of human societies, 'succeeding' here seems to clearly imply the meaning in terms of the 19th century evolutionary concept, namely, that 'cultures' succeed and replace each other in the evolutionary scale. Similarly, the last line of the above quota-tion suggests a borrowing of the 19th century historiography concepts and theories of migration, diffusion and movement of 'peoples' and 'races', from which we are not free yet. This 19th century conceptual framework is apparent in another statement with regard to the Sohan-Madrasian dichotomy of the lithic industries of the subcontinent; and is as follows: "The Singrauli basin near Mirzapur (U.P.) has been shown by the writer as a pivotal region for revealing a contact between two tool-traditions . . ."[21]

In this essay, there is also a noticeable use of the evolu-tionary concepts of culture and society but which are neither anywhere explicitly defined nor are they used in terms of the current social science understanding of process, change, etc. Thus, anthropological concepts are implicit in his statements, such as: "The data set forth above amply shows that a *pure mesolithic culture was being slowly transformed* into a microlithic pottery-using culture all over India. The existence of querns along with microliths at Langhnaj would particularly mean that the *original food-gatherers were being metamorphosed into the neolithic food-producers*".[22] The italicized lines (mine) in this statement clearly indicate not only the use of culture-historical terms but also some form of an evolutionary concept. But the criticism here is that once more the 19th century unilinear concepts have been utilized rather than the 20th century biological concept of organic evolution. In the earlier unilinear meaning of evolution the concepts, of 'process', 'change', etc. were not included in it because evolution was a conceptual sequence of abstract types. But now organic evolution refers to the actual process of change and not to any abstracted typological succession, i.e., "evolution is an actual process of change, not a classificatory characterization of sequences; that evolution consists of real events, so that evolutionary development is historical in the strictest and most literal sense".[23] It is worthwhile to note here that archaeologists even today in India neither specifically employ any of the currently valid concepts and analogies from the disciplines of biology, geology, history, anthropology, etc., nor do they appropriately and explicitly define and state the various terms and concepts that are borrowed and utilized.

Let us now examine another important work written after a decade of the above pioneering essay, in terms of theoretical 'progress'.

(2) *Prehistory and Protohistory in India and Pakistan*[24]: The approach followed by Prof. Sankalia in his monumental work has been clearly stated at the outset. "The aim has been to offer a critical review of the work done in these two branches of archaeology in this subcontinent during the last twenty years or so. *Naturally the concepts of prehistory and protohistory have been briefly examined and clarified as far as the current evidence permits. . . Though in any field of investigation or research, there should be some hypotheses to start with, yet the writer feels that these should legitimately follow when sufficient data have been gathered. The emphasis is therefore on careful collection of the material. Distribution charts and maps based on inadequate evidence are likely to mislead and give rise to false notions. . . the narrative is so planned that inferences or conclusions are not mixed up with any preconceived theories but the latter follow the main account and can be appraised independently and objectively*"[25] (Italics mine).

This opening statement which makes his approach quite clear is apparantly opposed to the problem-oriented approach (social science), which this monograph sets forth.   However, this book offers a good illustration of the commonmost form of carrying out research in history and archaeology in India.   There seems to be the general notion that an adequate description will produce an adequate explanation of why certain events happened. But from this premise arises that other common one in which temporal priority is often equated with a casual explanation. For example, if event or object A precedes B, then A is often considered to be the cause of B.   But facts — not even statistical figures — can ever speak or exist for themselves because whenever any facts are stated these have inevitably to be selected and described — whether consciously or unconsciously — within a frame of reference.   All adequate so-called 'factual' description always implies either an explicit or implicit hypothesis.   Thus, for instance, what was once considered to be an adequate description of archaeological evidence some twenty years ago is certainly not considered 'adequate' by us today because the earlier descriptions were given within frames of reference which are considered inadequate now.   Moreover, all responsible description is analysis of some sort because "a genuine scientific method has been inherent in all historical work, in all chronicling, in every argument used in jurisprudence, economics and linguistics.   There is no such thing as description completely devoid of theory.   Whether you reconstruct historic scenes, carry out field investigations in a savage tribe or a civilized community, analyse statistics, or make inferences from an archaeological monument or a prehistoric find. . . every statement and every argument has to be made in words, i.e., in concepts.   Each concept, in turn, is the result of a theory which declares that some facts are relevant and others, adventitious; that some factors determine the course of events and others are merely accidental by-play; that things happen as they do because personalities, masses and material agencies of the environment produced them. The hackneyed distinction between nomethetic and ideographic disciplines is a philosophical red herring which a simple consideration of what it means to observe, to reconstruct or state an historic fact ought to have been annihilated long ago".[26] Hence, this method of gathering the data first and asking questions afterwards is another unconsciously borrowed inheritance, and "is an old anthropological habit learned from justly revered masters, who adopted it because of the rush of ethnic and ethnographic change".[27]

Today, this lingering old habit is advocated not only by archaeologists but by even some of the eminent anthropologists of India who suggest that archaeologists should leave the business of theory to the social scientist and stick to the descriptive approach. There is, therefore, a sad lack of theorizing both in Indian history and archaeology since these disciplines have inherited an approach which consisted primarily of ideographic enquiries. But in order that an archaeologist may be better able to understand the past, it is no less important to carry out research on aspects which are of value for nomethetic enquiry. As a matter of fact, Prof. Sankalia does seem to be inclined towards seeking answers to some processual problems. For instance, he wonders why India should always be at the receiving end, and of the indigenous origin or diffusion of civilization to India. And, the explanation he gives is, "India has been, for the first time in her history, grouped into major linguistic states. Recognition has been given to a slow historical process. But the process was not only historical. It is related to a *certain extent* with the geographical (including the geological) features of the land. These have shaped not only her history, but prehistory and protohistory as well. . . We are thus up against the exact role of geography and environmental factors in the development of civilization. . . "[28] But beyond this brief suggested explanation there is no attempt to build up any useful elaborate framework. However, despite Prof. Sankalia's opening statement, he has not hesitated to borrow maps and geographical classifications which were formulated within a theoretical frame of reference by the Late Prof. B. Subbarao.[29]

Again, apart from the need to use some explicit frames of reference, archaeologists should at least avoid the confusion which would result in their using certain basic terms and definitions, by following some logic and methodology. Definitions in archaeology must be functional in the sense not only of keeping up with the currently valid logic and methodology but also in terms of the accepted generalizations about human society. In other words, since we deal with 'real' situations in terms of the 'true' statements of archaeological phenomena, the definitions have to be 'real' in the terms of probability constructs of the 'past-as-it-was'. Therefore, even any 'nominal' definitions of terms and concepts that a group of archaeologists agree to, arbitrarily, have to be defined and redefined from time to time with the changing historical and social science concepts and generalizations. Otherwise, as may be observed in the assorted definitions of prehistory in the statement given below, terms are liable to be used in a vague, redundant and abstract manner: "Prehistory means the history of a region, a country or a nation, people or race, before it took to or knew writing. This, like ordinary history, is not based on accounts of contemporary or later writers. *Hence prehistory is also defined as an account of illiterate or preliterate people. How is then the history of such an illiterate people or country known?* What are or can be its sources? In brief, anything that tells us its past history... Of all these sources, languages and linguistics, ethnography and ethnology, geography, geology, physical anthropology, flora and fauna, *we are concerned with archaeology alone* ... (it).... *means study of antiquities* ... *Prehistoric Archaeology then will deal with that period of time in India of which we have no legend, no tradition and no object, save stone (and bone) implements and remains of animals. This is not a very precise definition, but will, I find, serve our purpose. Briefly, then, prehistoric archaeology will comprise the various Stone Ages... Prehistory thus is a study of man's material as well as moral and spiritual progress...*"[30] (Italics mine).

Similarly, the use in archaeological literature of certain out-moded anthropological and sociological words and concepts is well exemplified by the following statement in this book: "*Economically, man was a savage, a hunter, though he might have subsisted largely on fruits, roots and grubs* during the early Palaeolithic and on the chase with the help of the bow and arrow or/ and spear during the Middle Palaeolithic. *Lastly, though so far only stone tools have been known of this stage of man's life and nothing else—man's other aspects of life—social, moral, religious— still the word 'culture' is applied to it,* because stone tools of certain type constantly recur in both the Stone Ages. These form a leading characteristic and give an inkling of the material culture of the man. Hence, instead of grouping the stone tools into simple "assemblages" or "industries", a term of greater significance and connotation, viz., culture, has been used. Strictly, only the former two terms are applicable"[31] (Italics mine).

Finally, the following statement by Prof. Sankalia vindicates our point of view of the state of archaeology in India today: "Work ahead. Both have still much to achieve. So far a mere skeleton sequence of cultures has been obtained in prehistory and protohistory, but the whole sociological background is missing... Thus in a sense, Indian prehistory is, where the European was in 1860. Only one redeeming feature is that in India stone implements are not being collected nor excavations conducted by untrained workmen and amateurs and momentous theories built on some selected material by scholars working on them... *In this work, therefore, care has been taken to use the old concepts and terms which have become standard, though found defective and fallacious, with as much precision as the data at our command allows us*"[32] (Italics mine).

Thus, without giving a fuller critical analysis of this book, the foregoing is fairly sufficient to illustrate the characteristic descriptive level of current Indian archaeological research. These studies seem to lack any effective intellectual operations that should be present in any academic discipline, and it is therefore for this reason that Indian archaeology has stayed at the 1860 level. However, it is incorrect of Prof. Sankalia to blame this state of affairs to the apathy of the "intellectual classes" in India, and to the mass illiteracy and poverty of India.[33] The remedy suggested by him is that interest in the things of the past may be created by popularizing archaeology through the media of newspapers, radio, etc. But, fundamentally, this is a wrong approach if the intention is to raise the status of archaeology to an intellectual discipline. "Archaeology must achieve the status as a university discipline that now it so sadly lacks by integration... And thus it will in the end attain a more secure public position than can be earned by sensational finds and even witty wireless programmes".[34]

Let us, now, examine the influence of this traditional approach in a recent university seminar on Indian prehistory. But it must be kept in mind that this criticism, to repeat, is with respect to the approach and the conceptual framework, and not the 'facts' that are stated in these essays, monographs and books. Therefore, in the descriptive tradition, tremendous work has been carried out in India and, perhaps, is of great value in this sense.

(3) *Indian Prehistory – 1964*[35]: It is normally expected of any university seminar to put forth hypotheses and theories because it is part and parcel of the academic 'business'. In this context, therefore, it is surprising to note the following limited aims and objectives of the present seminar: "This seminar had three main aims: To discuss a few important problems ... created

by intensive work ... during the last 15 years or so ... To
bring together the scholars — young and old — senior or junior,
working in this field,. ...*so that the latest data can be freely discussed, problems redefined and attempts made to face them.* .. The
third objective was to place before the scholars at large *the latest
happenings* in Indian prehistory and protohistory... It is hoped
that the publication of the proceedings of the seminar would help
to remove this deliberate neglect of Indian prehistory... *the
themes chosen were not very specific, but broad, so that we could
attack them from different points of view.* .. *Secondly, only those
scholars were invited to participate in the seminar who either as
field workers or organizers or authors had intimate first-hand
knowledge of the subjects selected for discussion.* .. *Without doing
considerable work, no purpose would be served in holding similar
seminars in the near future.* .. *The other urgent need is to disse-
minate the knowledge already acquired in several aspects of pre and
protohistory* to schools, colleges and educated laymen. Otherwise, we shall remain isolated in our ivory towers"[36] (Italics
mine). Similarly, the following headings of various sections,
in this seminar, clearly reflect the descriptive approach to the
problems of Indian archaeology, and suggest that no attempt
was made to break away from the old mould of the 19th century
concepts: *"Is Soan a separate culture?* ... Some Problems
Concerning Pleistocene Stratigraphy of India... Middle Stone
Age Cultures in India and Pakistan... Mesolithic Phase...
Neolithic Problem... *The Indus Civilization: Its origin, Authors,
Extent and Chronology* ... *Relationship of Indian Chalcolithic
Cultures with West Asia* ..."[37] (Italics mine).

On the discussion of the 'Neolithic Problem in India', the
typical traditional approach is well illustrated by the following
statement of one of the participants: "In almost all recent literature dealing with the 'Neolithic' one finds too much stress on
the economy which is gradually overshadowing the technical
aspects of culture... *Too much stress on economy, which at least*

in the case of India is nothing more than a drawing-room specula-
tion, will lead us to abandon divisions in prehistory like the Palaeo-
lithic, Mesolithic, Neolithic, Copper Age and Bronze Age, etc. which
are based on technical changes evidenced by convincing archaeo-
logical data. . . Chalcolithic. . . This stage, in fact, is a transitional
phase between the Neolithic Barbarism and the Urbanization"[38]
(Italics mine).

However, on the other hand, the statements of some of the
members of the Archaeological Survey of India who, incidentally, are also kept busy with the problems of looking
after the repair, conservation and preservation of monuments,
reflect a definite attempt to adopt certain recent trends in
archaeological research.   The following is one such statement:
"Gordon Childe emphasised the functional economic significance of the event when he introduced the concept 'Neolithic
Revolution'. Still more recently, Braidwood developed a
new terminology to replace the older typological terminology
(Palaeolithic, Mesolithic and Neolithic) and the evolutionary
terms of the culture-historians . . . is illustrative of the general
growth of anthropological thinking in archaeology".[39]

Finally, there is another observation which may be seen in
this seminar report, and in many other reports of Indian archaeology. It is this, that interpretations are frequently based on
conjectural and imaginative statements rather than on
either any social science generalizations or ethnographic fact.
These reconstructions may be referred to as 'pseudo-historical',
'pseudo-causal' explanations, and it is this fact which has also
prevented archaeological (historical) reconstruction from be-
coming truly academic and sophisticated. Thus, one of the
best ways to approach any archaeological problem would be to
recognize that there are two relatively distinct levels on which
any reconstruction or theorizing might be attempted. The first
level is the one closest to ethnographic facts in terms of which
the immediate conceptual framework may be formulated, and

the observed archaeological phenomena (activities) described and interpreted. The second level within which such recons- truction may be carried out is that of general theory because archaeological phenomena in this case may be used to serve illustrative and demonstrative purposes as the main concern of the theorist would be to discern lines and patterns—generaliza- tions—in his subject-matter. The second level is well known in most other disciplines, but even ethnographic knowledge is often neglected in Indian archaeological reconstructions. Thus, for instance, both ethnographic knowledge and general anthro- pology teach us that in the typological method of Indian archaeology traits are treated independently and arbitrarily, and that they are shuffled and reshuffled in the course of 'historical explanations violating the cardinal principle of the inter-connectedness of all elements of culture'. This specially is the case with the crucially important ceramic and stone tool classifications which do not take into account the 'real' or 'functional' criteria of the definitions. The following ethno- graphic example from an Australian aboriginal tribe might better illustrate this stress on the 'total' or 'functional' viewpoint:

"They are, of course, nomads-hunters and foragers who grow nothing, build nothing, and stay nowhere long. They make almost no physical mark on the environment. Even in areas which are still inhabited, it takes a knowledgeable eye to detect their recent presence. Within a matter of weeks, the roughly cleared campsite may be erased by sun, rains, and wind. After a year or two there may be nothing to suggest that the country was ever inhabited. Until one stumbles on a few old flint tools, a stone quarry, a shell midden, a rock painting,... one may think the land had never known the touch of man... They move about, carrying their scant possessions, in small bands of any- thing from ten to sixty persons. Each band belongs to a given locality. A number of bands, anything from three or four upto twelve or fifteen, depending on the fertility of the area make up a 'tribe'. A tribe is usually a language or dialect group which thinks of itself as having a certain unity of common speech and shared customs. The tribes range in size from a few hundred to a few thousand souls.

"One rarely sees a tribe as a formed entity. It comes together and lives as a unit only for a great occasion — a feast, a corroboree, a hunt, an initiation, or a formal duel. After a few days, at most weeks, it breaks up again into smaller bands or sections of bands... These parties rove about their family locality, or by agreement the territories of immediate neighbours. They do not wander aimlessly, but to a purpose, and in tune with the seasonal food supply. One can almost plot a year of their life in terms of movement towards the places where honey, yams, grass seeds, eggs, or some other food staple, is in bearing and ready for eating.

"The uncomplex visible routine, and the simple segmentation are very deceptive. It took well over half a century for Europeans to realize that behind the outward show was an inward structure of surprising complexity. It was a century before any real understanding of this structure developed".[40]

It is thus obvious from this brief ethnographic example that in the currently used typologies in Indian prehistory the mere knowledge of stone tool technology is insufficient, reflecting a very low and incomplete level of reconstruction of prehistoric human societies. There is, therefore, all the more reason why archaeologists must always observe and classify archaeological evidence in terms of 'living societies', specially because artifacts are referential and can be functional only in terms of the 'socio-cultural' context and process. One cannot overlook the fact of the dynamics of cultural process that is implied in the artifacts because they are the result of an immense multitude of actions and interactions of human beings, and are part of a process that does not take place at random. But it must be borne in mind that the concept of 'function'

mentioned here is not the same as it is current in Indian archaeology, where it usually means a simple description such as a fork
is used for picking or a spoon is used for scooping, etc., because
this description does not supply us information as to how a fork or
a spoon is related to table manners in different socio-cultural
contexts. Thus, as a methodological indictment, this simple
concept of 'function' discloses the low 'intellectual' level of
Indian archaeology.

III

Finally, to conclude and summarize, the following points
may be observed.

(1) Indian archaeology continues to be haunted by the basic
problems of definition. As in some immature sciences and
humanities its vocabulary is derived from various sources such
as aesthetics, psychology, art-history, history, biology, natural
sciences and anthropology. Some of the key terms and concepts continue to evoke wide differences in meaning and provoke
heated controversies. This is partly because the community
of archaeologists, in general, is not a 'natural language community', who do not share a common academic or socio-
cultural background. The effect of this is revealed in the statements that characteristically show, consciously or unconsciously,
extra-scientific considerations. For instance, when some historians and archaeologists have tried to prove that India was
the original land of the Indo-Aryans, or that the Harappa
civilization was 'Aryan'. Similarly, many Western scholars
and their Indian followers have sought to trace the origins of
almost all traits and cultures from the West, while the influences
from the East on Indian 'culture and civilization' have been
ignored.[41]

(2) In Indian archaeology may also be noted the presence of
what might be called the obsession with universality. Thus, for

example, many choose European terminology and feel perplexed when it does not seem applicable to the entire Indian subcontinent, or, if new generalized terms like the Early, Middle and Late Stone Ages are suggested it is taken for granted that these terms will be universally applicable, both temporally and spatially.

(3) It is obvious, then, while concepts and definitions cannot take the place of empirical inquiry, in the absence of hypotheses, concepts and definitions, there can be no inquiry. For instance, it is a definition, either ostensive or nominal, which designates the phenomena to be investigated. Nevertheless, as has been shown above, Indian archaeology has continued to follow its untrained predecessors. As a consequence, today it has also led our younger colleagues and students "to neglect somewhat those elemental phases of human existence, just because they seem to be obvious and generally human, non-sensational and non-problematic. And yet it is clear that a selection made on the principle of exotic, sensational or outlandish divergencies from the universally human run of behaviour is itself not a scientific selection".[42]

(4) Lastly, it is hoped that the reader will bear in mind that the criticism in this chapter was primarily from the viewpoint of theoretical 'progress' and not the 'factual' contents of the various works. This criticism had to be stated because many archaeologists and anthropologists in India do not consider it a fit business of archaeology to indulge in the subtleties of concepts, definitions, etc. They would rather continue to restrict its business to the collection and description of its data within a chronological framework. This is precisely one of the reasons why in the various archaeological reports, accurate though these may be, the definition of 'A' in one monograph is 'B' in another and there has been no concerted effort to get over this preliminary stage of standardization of the basic terms and definitions. But this criticism should not be construed to mean that

it is just a matter of semantics or of seeking arbitrary agreement in vocabulary. The formulation of precise words, terminologies and concepts is the first step towards building hypotheses, both prior to fieldwork as well as subsequent to it. It would be a truism to state that words reflect concepts and, therefore, definitions are conceptual devices for controlling the function of words. But, as has been noted, theoretical formulations are either left to the anthropologists, historians, etc., or there is a great reliance on vague dogmatically asserted intuitions instead of the most cautiously formulated inferences which would have been in order.

NOTES AND REFERENCES

1. See references given in *Cultural Forum*, December 1961, a special number on Indian Archaeology's centenary, New Delhi (Indian Council for Cultural Affairs), and *Ancient India*, No. 9, 1953, Special Jubilee number (1902-1952) of the Archaeological Survey of India, New Delhi.
2. Roy, Sourindranath, in *Ancient India*, No. 9, 1953, p. 4.
3. Ibid., p. 5.
4. Ibid.
5. Ibid., p. 6.
6. Ibid., pp. 7-8.
7. Ibid., p. 9.
8. Ibid., p. 10.
9. Ghosh, A., in *Cultural Forum*, December 1961, p. 6.
10. Roy, S., in op. cit., 1953, p. 13.
11. Ghosh, A., in op. cit., 1961, p. 7.
12. Roy, S., in op. cit., 1953, p. 21.
13. Ibid., p. 27.
14. Ghosh, A., in *Ancient India*, No. 9, 1953, p. 31.
15. Ghosh, in op. cit., 1961, p. 11.
16. Ghosh, in op. cit., 1953, p. 42.
17. Ibid.
18. Ibid., p. 44.
19. Krishnaswamy, V. D., in *Ancient India*, No. 9, 1953, pp. 53-79.
20. Ibid., p. 62.
21. Ibid., p. 61.

22. Ibid., p. 74.
23. Murdock, George Peter, "Evolution in Social Organization", *Evolution: A Centennial Appraisal*, ed. Betty J. Meggars, 1959, p. 129.
24. Sankalia, H. D., *Prehistory and Protohistory in India and Pakistan*, University of Bombay, 1962.
25. Ibid., p. ix.
26. Malinowski, B., *Scientific Theory of Culture*, 1960, pp. 7-8.
27. Howells, William W., "Population Distances: Biological, Linguistic, Geographical and Environmental", *Current Anthropology*, Vol. 7, 5, Chicago, 1966, p. 531.
28. Sankalia, H. D., op cit., 1962, pp. i, viii.
29. Subbarao, B., *Personality of India*, M. S. University of Baroda, 1958.
30. Sankalia, H. D., op. cit., 1962, pp. ix, x, xii.
31. Ibid., p. xix.
32. Ibid., p. xviii.
33. Ibid.
34. Childe, V. G., in *Bulletin of the Institute of Archaeology*, I, 1958, p. 8.
35. Misra, V. N. and Mate, M. S., eds, *Indian Prehistory – 1964*, Deccan College, Poona, 1965.
36. Sankalia, H. D., in ibid., pp. vii-ix.
37. Ibid., p. xiii.
38. Mahapatra, G. C., in ibid., p. 103.
39. Thapar, B. K., in ibid., p. 107.
40. Stanner, W.E.H., "The Dreaming, an Australian World View", *Cultural and Social Anthropology*, ed. Peter Hammond, 1964. pp. 288-298.
41. Subbarao, B., "Studies in some Cultural Impacts at the Formative Stages of India's Culture", *Asian History Congress*, 1961, Azad Bhavan, New Delhi (Mimeographed).
42. Malinowski, B., op. cit., 1960, p. 72.

HISTORY, ARCHAEOLOGY
AND ANTHROPOLOGY

History may be defined as the sequential description of the events of nature or human society. But, as natural events cannot be equated with human events, one distinguishes between natural history and human history. Therefore, all human events are fundamentally historical and the discipline of archaeology in this sense belongs to history. It has been so not only in operational practice but also in philosophical theory. However, strictly speaking, the discipline of History is generally limited to the study of literate societies because its research is based on the evidence of written documents which are, in the main, highly personalized because from these one may not only sometimes infer unique events but also the individual person playing his part. But restricting the study of History to the study of documented societies is only a matter of conceptual and academic convenience since, philosophically, History is coterminus with mankind. Hence, the limitations of the fields of archaeology and History are only a matter of academic convenience and have very little to do with the real situation. For instance, it is hard to imagine that there was a sharp dividing line in the socio-cultural organization between the preliterate societies and those with a knowledge of writing which must have coexisted specially during a time when literacy was prevalent only in some urban areas. There was most probably a long period of gradual change in the socio-cultural organization before the non-literate societies turned into elementary literate societies, and finally into fully literate societies. Therefore, whenever archaeological means are employed during a period when the help of documentary evidence is available, this form of historical reconstruction has been termed as *text-aided archaeology*. It has the advantage over the archaeology of the pre-literate and non-literate societies of having at least the broad outlines concerned already worked out by non-archaeological means.

In the past, in India, *text-aided archaeology*, as the continuation of the 18th-19th century aesthetic approach, had mainly helped the art-historian, the student of architecture and numismatics in the acquisition of objects. But in recent years it has also helped to uncover ancient historical sites, to check stylistically art-objects in datable contexts and to recover additional documents. However, for the purposes of writing culture-history, specially from the socio-cultural viewpoint, the correlation of documentary evidence to the archaeological one is not easy in India since much of the documentation is mixed with myths and legends of the popular tradition. Moreover, at times, these documents tend to overemphasise or exaggerate religious and personal views, or they may deal exclusively with economic transactions. Then, again, the interpretation of a document frequently involves the problem of verification of references that mention other non-literate tribes. (For example, there is the intricate problem of correlating the various ceramic groups such as the Painted-Grey-Ware one to the tribes of the Puranic literary traditions or to specific groups of the Aryans that are mentioned in the texts.) Nevertheless, it is now also fairly well known that *text-aided archaeology* can, as one learns from examples in the Euro-American context, help a great deal in writing socio-economic and socio-cultural histories. It has enabled one to complete significant items that are not available in documentary evidence. For instance, information such as the domestication of plants and animals, about animal husbandry and agriculture, about the preparation of food and drink, textiles and medicines, and specially about ancient technology (because skills were generally handed down without being recorded from generation to generation). *Text-aided archaeology* has also illuminated the relationship of the community to its natural environment and its trade and commercial relationship by identifying various materials and their sources.[1]

However, it is perhaps better known that the main sphere of archaeological activity is in the preliterate period of human history. This "pre-historic" period of the study of the past human events may, preferably, be termed as *text-free history* rather than text-free archaeology. But the methods of recovery of the artistic and mundane objects, by means of extremely refined scientific procedures, of both *text-aided archaeology* and *text-free history* are much the same. The latter, however, is totally dependent upon archaeological evidence and archaeological reasoning for the knowledge of human activity and human achievements. It largely employs, as stated in the Introduction, techno-economic models, following the temper of our age and restricted by the nature of its evidence. At any rate, in India, both these subdivisions of archaeology proceed, after the recovery of the remains, to describe and categorize the evidence and place it in a chronological order. Finally, the research worker develops a scheme of evolutionary sequence or hypotheses of the spread, migration of trait/traits which are equated often with 'cultures', 'peoples', 'linguistic groups', 'races', etc. But this descriptive approach, as has been stated previously, employs conceptual schemes that are related to only two sets of questions. These are the 'when' and 'where' questions of the traditional Historical approach which developed out of the method and habit of analysing documentary evidence. However, the prevalence of this approach in India is also partly the result of our inheriting the tradition of the British historical schools as against the Continental and American schools of archaeology which have always retained close ties with anthropology and the other social sciences. In America, this was the case because of the historical circumstance of the confrontation of the European immigrant scholars to both the living aboriginal societies and their prehistoric sites in that region. Thus, the social science-oriented schools of archaeology have had somewhat different questions to raise about archaeological evidence than has been the case with the historical or historiography-oriented schools, such as in India.

Now, the problem here is not whether one ought to place archaeology with History or with anthropology because, admittedly, History, archaeology and anthropology have, in general, developed with freedom and divergence in techniques, subject-matter, objectives and perspectives. Therefore, they are different academic disciplines, and have been quite unlike each other in both origin and intention. But it cannot be overlooked that all three disciplines deal with the same broad subject-matter, except that archaeology and anthropology do not generally deal with History's specific and unique events which are not easily amenable to generalizations. Moreover, it is archaeology which, of necessity, has to deal with evidence which comprises 'mass phenomenal' objects that are able to survive only because these objects were socially accepted in a given society.[2] Therefore, the 'anonymous' evidence of archaeology is much more amenable to generalizations than is the evidence of History which is compiled from the unique events of documentary evidence. This implies that it will be very fruitful to approach the evidence of archaeology also in terms of the social sciences (anthropology) than to approach it merely by the historical method. This viewpoint is further enforced by the fact that although the evidence of archaeology is of a limited nature (since it usually lacks the direct documentary evidence of History's unique events), yet it is precisely because of this limitation that it becomes of considerable significance for us to view it in terms of certain generalizations of the social sciences. Thus, there is not only potential but actual inter-dependence of archaeology and anthropology because both deal with problems that are concerned with general rather than specific human interaction.

The objective before us, therefore, is one of achieving a proper balance by laying greater emphasis on the anthropological approach to the study of different archaeological problems than has hitherto been the case in India. There is a great need to do this today because it alone will enable Indian archaeology to deal with questions relating to the 'how' and 'why' of past human societies. It is only in this manner that archaeology will then be able to make generalizing statements about processes and regularities of past human societies and, thereby, not only contribute to its own growth but also contribute towards the general understanding of human societies. But if archaeology in India has up till now not formulated any generalities from its data, it is because the traditional approach of History does not require it to look at the material relics within the socio-cultural context. It is certainly not because such formulations are not possible, but because it is always easy to put together a logical scheme of events since this does not require any explanation of the problems related to the 'how' and 'why' of events. On the other hand, answers to the latter require, at least, a basic theoretical social science knowledge of the nature, structure and function of human societies. The understanding of these and other processes is not as simple as it is often made out in the literature of Indian archaeology.

But it now seems obvious that we cannot for long remain without any models, frames of reference and some abstract theoretical aspects if only in order to tie up our discipline with the other allied fields, specially anthropology. Moreover, Indian archaeology must become an intellectual discipline because it cannot any more continue to use vague concepts, such as the 'shreds and patches' or 'diffusion' theory, or that of 'material culture', etc. Again, for instance, the concept of 'culture' and 'cultural activity' which is of obvious crucial relevance for archaeology is seldom clearly defined. But if Indian archaeology has not cared to concern itself with the nature and dynamics of culture, it is not because there is a lack of any special abilities, but simply because this demands a high order of anthropological sophistication. It is because of this sad neglect of cultural anthropology that the vast body of facts of Indian archaeology, which have been delineated into a historical sequence, are generally explained in isolation as the mere descriptive record of an existential series of human events. Therefore, the attention of Indian archaeology has been chiefly paid to the definition of 'cultural' units through the classification of artifacts and the chronological ordering of the units and artifact classes concentrating on typological features of value for classification. But if it is realized that there are more problems contained in the material of archaeology than those which are considered at present, then its range of consideration may even be broadened to include the nature of man and considerations of process and destiny. By doing this, it will become necessary, in due course, to broaden the scope of the basic definitions which are used in archaeology. In this context, it would, therefore, be better to exemplify our view by briefly examining the concept of 'culture' in archaeology and anthropology.

Archaeologists have used 'culture' in a restricted sense, defining it as an assemblage of associated traits that recur repeatedly. This is because the material remains of archaeological evidence are in fact the only symbols for distinguishing 'cultures' which are identified by one or more diagnostic traits. The picture that is thus built up is one of many fragments observed at different places and at different times. The anthropologist's conception of culture, on the other hand, is much more comprehensive. It comprises all the manifestations of human behaviour that do not result from innate reflexes or instincts but everything that men derive from nurture, from human society. The anthropologist looks at 'society' and 'culture' as interwoven aspects of a complex phenomenon of human groups, and from his evidence he attempts to formulate certain generalizations of recurrent processes. It is within this comprehensive anthropological manner of viewing the evidence that an archaeologist (historian) should also look at his evidence because it is equally important for us to understand the dynamics of past societies, as far as such generalities and processes can be extricated from the material evidence. It is, of course, considerably simpler to understand culture by the form it takes rather than by any definition, and to deal with its actual manifestations rather than with its abstract forms. But it is for this very simple reason we find that archaeological 'societies' or 'cultures', which have generally been reconstructed on the basis of a great deal of discussion on type fossils, seem to become mere assemblages of lifeless accidental types. It is because of this narrow view that archaeologists generally tend to become too absorbed in minute details and overlook the 'macro-dynamic' aspects of 'culture', forgetting that the surviving accidental types and the various missing constituents are interrelated elements of a functional whole. It is, therefore, no surprise to note the partial archaeological reconstructions that are largely the result of the use of the restricted archaeological definition of 'culture', even this is taken for granted. But, by restricting archaeological interpretation to this working definition of culture it has been tacitly assumed that little more is possible than listing and chronicling. It must, however, be realized that the restricted use of definitions and concepts not only limits the freedom of our thought processes but also the intelligent use of the refinements in the techniques that are increasingly at the disposal of the archaeologist.

Hence, it is important for archaeology to allow the use of comprehensive anthropological and other social science definitions which will make it possible to open new vistas for broader interpretations, through further intricate developments in the natural and physical sciences. The use of such comprehensive definitions will enable both the archaeologist and the anthropologist to carry out temporal cross-cultural studies within a common set of currently valid concepts. It is in this manner that archaeology will also be able to contribute to the growth of certain social sciences because although, ideally speaking, anthropology deals with 'cultures' as such, yet it cannot adequately do so without the help of archaeological knowledge in order to achieve its objectives of writing the history of human culture and society. But unlike the anthropologist who can afford to study his recent — or comparatively recent — societies in fragments because he can go back into the field to restudy them, the archaeologist simply cannot afford to do so because once his evidence is excavated from its *in situ* context, any chances of reconstructing the spatial and temporal 'functional' interrelationships of the various relics which have been extricated are lost for ever. Therefore, the archaeologist has to be extremely cautious while exploring and excavating because he must bear in mind the total 'socio-cultural' frame of reference prior to the commencement of fieldwork. The reason why this 'total' framework is important is that the fact of events is implicit in the material evidence, and implicit in the facts of events is the process of change. Therefore, whatever be the limitation of the evidence, archaeological societies are dynamic, and not static. Hence, it is imperative to remember several aspects and considerations of society and culture, such as the use of distributional and settlement patterns, functional relationships of tool clusters, etc., prior to fieldwork.

It is, of course, not being stated that Indian archaeologists do not attempt any technological and economic reconstructions, or for that matter it is not the intention to undermine the tremendous work that Indian archaeology is carrying out. However, the fact remains that traditional archaeologists do very often justify the legitimacy of their old approach because of the limitation of archaeological evidence. Therefore, the intention here is simply to map out a road for the 'progress' of Indian archaeology which, somehow, seems to feel shy of adopting new ideas, concepts and schemes.[3] Archaeologists simply cannot ignore the dynamic aspect of human societies which in fact is represented in the material evidence of archaeology. It is in this sense, therefore, that the archaeologist cannot but help being considered as an anthropologist (even if the historian wishes to be excluded).

In short, archaeology (history) as a discipline that attempts to understand past events of human societies belongs both to the humanities and the social sciences and, as is known, it extensively utilizes the help of the natural and physical sciences for the recovery of its evidence. Hence, it is only by means of emphasising the integrative inter-disciplinary approach and by developing a philosophy of its own that archaeology will be able to contribute towards helping mankind understand itself better. We must remember, that the broad field of enquiry for the archaeologist is the 'human phenomenon' and human condition, and not merely the task of being an intelligent chronicler.

II

It will now be appropriate to illustrate this viewpoint by presenting some archaeological evidence in terms of one of the anthropological models which, for instance, could be employed for prehistoric research in India. This is a model of the prehistoric cultural levels in India, as far as it was possible to do this from the meagre evidence that was available, and it has been adopted from Braidwood's scheme of the conceptual model of subsistence settlement types.[4] The following broad sequence is a generalized illustrative one without any attempt to fix a predetermined order so that, whenever the need arises to present regional sequences on the basis of this model, specific terms will then have to be devised.

I. Food Gathering Stage.
    A. Food Gathering era with sub-eras (Period: Early Stone Age).
    (1) Naturally determined mammalian subsistence and free wandering level. Tools fashioned but not yet standardized. E.g., Pre-Sohan(?).
    (2) Food gathering and free wandering begin to be significantly determined. Tools of the earliest standardized tradition. E.g., Early Sohan, Early Madrasian.
    (3) Elemental restricted wandering hunting; regional restriction and variety. Artifactual hints of intentional burials. A moral order ? Sexual division of labour, with men hunting and women collecting plants and insect food, already existent ? E.g., Late Sohan flake industries, developed Handaxe, Final Madrasian.
    B. Food Collecting era with sub-eras.
    (1) Technological early level (Period: Middle Stone Age). Selection, hunting, and seasonal collecting patterns for restricted wandering types of groups. Typological variety; regional restriction of any given industry(?) although generalized tool preparation still widespread. E.g., 'Series II' of Nevasa, etc.
    (2) Technological later level (Period: Late Stone Age, includes (3) below). Intensified hunting and collecting, season-bound activities. E.g., The non-geometric industries.
    (3) Highly specialized environments which allow semi-permanent to permanent sedentary types of groups. Extends to the present ethnological groups. E.g., Geometric microlithic industries.
II. Food Producing Stage. (Period: Food Producing-'Neolithic'-Age).
    (1) Incipient cultivation. Animal domestication in some regions. Restricted wandering to semi-permanent

settlements. Experimental era difficult to concep-
tualize. E.g., Langhnaj (?).

(2) The primary village farming community in which a
marked proportion of the dietary intake is produced
food, and in this these are self-sufficient. E.g., The
'polished stone-celt' communities.

(3) Expanded village farming communities, permanent
settlements and secondary communities. Increasing
cultural contact and diffusion of traits. Technologies
would include the blade industries, specialized pottery,
basketry and also traces of copper-working with
regional variations. It is the beginning of the break-
up of the self-sufficing aspect although the villages
remain self-contained.

III. The next stage is a transitional one and the picture
becomes complex because the differential cultural development
in the diverse 'geographic' regions of India becomes
very evident. There is varied culture-historical evidence
that includes urbanization. The archaeological evidence now
is not restricted to the techno-economic aspects as in the previous two levels. Therefore, now, the evidence is amenable
to the socio-cultural analysis of defining this culture-
historical level.

The problems related to this level (III) being complex and
lengthy will be discussed in the next chapter because what one
has to attempt now is to discover a finite number of socio-cultural processes hidden within the innumerable large and minute
facts and details which are known to the archaeologist, either
about the Harappan society or any other 'culture' of this period.
Moreover, this kind of analysis requires the problem-oriented
many-sided questioning mentality in order to discover the various socio-cultural 'facts', which are seldom available in the im-
mediately apprehensible and perceptible characteristics of forms
and numbers. What 'facts' happen to be, always depend upon

the questions that have been put because there are always different aspects of reality reflected even in a limited body of archaeological evidence. For example, the evidence at the interrelated sites of Kotla Nihang Khan, Rupar, Bara, etc., has chiefly been classified on the basis of ceramic typologies into pre-Harappan, Harappan and late or degenerate Harappan. But this kind of inference, correct as it may be, could possibly as well have been of a different order. For instance, the evidence at these different settlements might as well be seen in terms of small villages and towns which represent different socio-economic groups of one contemporary 'culture' or 'society', instead of interpreting the variations in ceramic typologies only in terms of chronological or evolutionary levels. In other words, the inferences of the spatial 'functional' interrelationships of archaeological evidence in a particular area are of no less importance than the temporal ones which archaeologists frequently do consider. Again, for instance, the six ceramic groups at Kalibangan from A to F, which have been correctly described by Thapar[5] according to form and style, could also be interpreted as representing different social levels or social groups of a 'culture', rather than only representing an evolutionary series or even different 'ethnic' endogamous groups, as is generally done. Similarly, even in an evolutionary temporal sequence the socio-cultural implications of the evidence may be differently inferred, such as perhaps in the case of the evidence from Atranjikhera.[6] Here, the persistence and displacement in the proportions of the ceramic evidence of the Red-ware from the different levels might as well suggest some sort of social change for displacement, etc. in the hierarchy of the different groups in that 'society' or 'culture'.

The lines of inference and interpretation suggested above are not new because these are already being carried out in Europe and in America by certain intricate methods of analysis, in order to interpret ceramic and other archaeological evidence in socio-cultural terms. However, this does not mean that all archaeological evidence is amenable to such socio-anthropological analysis and classification. But in archaeological interpretation one must at least distinguish between different traits and trait complexes at different levels of analysis, i.e., some traits may be of value for sociological classification while others may be useful for historical purposes, and still others for mere aesthetic or artistic value, etc. This form and method of analysis of interpretation will only become possible when we, in India, begin to use the laws and generalizations of the social sciences, and lay less stress on the unique aspects of traits and trait-complexes as if the different traits are the results of chance agglomerations, or are dispersed entirely by diffusion, etc. Thus, it will be more fruitful for Indian archaeologists to have a combined historical and anthropological approach or, what may more appropriately be called the combined cultural and social anthropological approach. "The approach of cultural anthropology is *holistic* in that it is concerned with all aspects of human belief and behaviour: it is historical in its stress on the factor of time as relevant to an understanding of human experience: *humanistic* in that its point of reference includes the individual, even as he is being shaped by them. Social anthropology, in contrast, is *specialized*, in that it concentrates on the social aspect of group life; *synchronic*, since its aim is the analysis of relationships within a given group on a single time plane; and *structural*, in that it is primarily concerned with institutional arrangement . . .".[7]

Thus, to conclude and summarize, the problem facing Indian archaeology is the application of this combined approach, specially an emphasis on the anthropological one because that is an aspect which has so far not been applied to Indian archaeological studies. The anthropological emphasis of this monograph is deliberate because Indian archaeology, following the traditional approach, has been content to divide its evidence into major and minor sequences which are based on certain stylistic ceramic forms and designs, and it has not been able to provide any clues as to any 'functional' interrelationships. But the latter can only become possible when certain archaeological problems are described and defined in terms of socio-cultural systems, specially prior to fieldwork because after the material evidence is recovered many important inferences are not possible. However, by this sociological and anthropological inference is not meant the simple earlier interpretation of the evidence into burials, houses, etc., which has been somewhat obvious to the archaeologists even by traditional methods. The task, therefore, before us "is not one of abstracted classification but is concerned with real people, real cultures, in real environments. It is heavily speculative and inferential, of course, but it must be less abstracted and categorical and more concrete and complicated. . . Real people in a real society do not fill their time by preferring in the sphere of technology at one time, social organization at another, and ideology still later. Furthermore, they are in close association with, and subjected to, the environment".[8]

However, the subject at hand is a difficult one (with regard to the last level (III) of the above scheme) and an attempt will be made in the next main chapter to understand it in terms of the perpetuation and persistence of some Harappan systems and institutions. This will be carried out within the pertinent context of the Harappan contribution to the main stream of the formative stages of Indian civilization.[9] The arguments used will be inferential and inductive, and this attempt may be called speculative, but it is not speculative in the traditional 'pseudo-historical' sense because it has been tempered by laws and generalizations of certain social sciences, as far as it was possible to discover these from the currently available archaeological and historical literature. Thus, it is hoped that not only will the data for this level (period) be held together in a manner which will render it more intelligible, but also that it will exemplify our viewpoint of what has been enunciated above with regard to the study of archaeology in India. In the next chapter there is, however, a tacit assumption that the reader is somewhat familiar with the general archaeological literature of India. Therefore, there will be no elaborate details of archaeological evidence except where it is necessary to illustrate our viewpoint.

NOTES AND REFERENCES

1. Clarke, Grahme, *Prehistoric Europe: The Economic Basis*, London, 1952.
2. Childe, V. Gordon, *Society and Knowledge*, London, 1956.
3. This was the case, for instance, in 1961 at the first Asian Archaeology Conference held in New Delhi. The author had read a paper incorporating the Stone Age terminology within a culture-historical framework. But this simple suggestion was not acceptable to the majority of the Committee, excepting Professor Braidwood.
4. Braidwood, R. J., "Levels in Prehistory: A Model for the Reconsideration of the Evidence", *The Evolution of Man*, Vol. II, ed. Sol Tax, Chicago, 1960, pp. 143-152.
5. Thapar, B. K., in *Indian Prehistory — 1964*, eds. Misra and Mate, 1965, p. 136.
6. Gour, R. C., in ibid., pp. 142-145, 167-168.
7. Herskovits, Melville J., "For the Historical Approach in Anthropology: A Critical Case", in *Cultural and Social Anthropology*, ed. Peter Hammond, 1964, pp. 436-443.
8. Service, Elman R., *Primitive Social Organization*, Random House, New York, 1964, p. 26.
9. This has been very well stressed by Walter A. Fairservis, Jr. "The Origin, Character, and Decline of an Early Civilization", *American Museum Novitates*, New York, No. 2302, 1967.

FORMATIVE PERIOD OF INDIAN CIVILIZATION

INTRODUCTION

Professional students of culture and civilization have formulated various conceptual models for the scientific and scholarly understanding of India and, depending upon the orientation of the scholar concerned, have stressed one aspect in favour of the other because of the vastness and complexity of the material involved. Hence, different methods and themes of inquiry for understanding India have been formulated by the historian, political and social scientist, art-historian, etc. But it is largely as a result of the interpretations carried out by scholars whose field of study is Ancient India, along with some others, that civilization in India has been characterized in its idealized intellectual and spiritual traditions. This is most probably because of the heavy reliance by these scholars upon literary sources of tradition which either narrate the story of the elite (literati) or their abstract philosophical commentaries. The impact of this idealized view has been so very great that the spiritual aspects of Indian civilization have completely overshadowed the sober and substantial approach such as that of the social scientist whose path has not always been recognized. "Histories of philosophic thought, of political ideology, of artistic creation have only too often neglected the fact that any form of individual inspiration becomes cultural reality if it can capture the public opinion of a group, implement the inspirations with material means of its expression, and thus become embodied into an institution".[1]

Similarly, the interpretations of archaeology depend a great deal upon the imperishable surviving material of a human society, so that the definition of civilization now is in terms of its emergence in an evolutionary sequence. It has been identified by the presence of such features as monumentality of art and architecture, town-planning, metal tools and weapons, cultivation of plants and domestication of animals, specialization of crafts such as textiles, manufacture of bricks and pots, etc.[2] If these defined features are translated into sociological terms, it means that the organization of the emergent 'civilized' society is now on a basis of residence, in place of or on top of a basis of kinship, and there is also the emergence of full-time specialists in the urban areas, with a privileged 'ruling' class who lives by the institution of tribute or taxation that results in the central accumulation of 'capital'. The latter, in turn, accelerates the development of other socio-economic institutions which enable the possibility of a greatly expanded internal and foreign trade.

On the other hand, the cultural anthropologist's approach to the study of civilizations has been very aptly expressed as follows: "Modern anthropology offers to the study of the cultural history of civilizations two important insights: (1) that every culture is a complex and composite growth which derives most of its component elements from its own past or has borrowed these from other cultures; and (2) that every culture tends to develop a distinctive organization, coherent and self-consistent, which tends to absorb new elements whether borrowed or indigenous, and to reshape them to accord with its own patterns . . . those two insights are not in opposition but are complementary and can be combined. . . But in spite of their interest in 'culture wholes', anthropologists have shown marked reluctance to concern themselves with the larger culture wholes ordinarily called civilization . . . mere size . . . acts as a deterrent . . . when anthropological endeavours have taken on broader scope, they have inclined to lack depth and factual substantiality, remaining spotty or impressionistic. . . Civilizations resemble organic classes in being natural systems. That is, they can be said to possess both a structure and a content within this structure . . . the structure and content of civilizations do change . . . institutional events they might be called. . . no civilization is ever actually static.   It always flows. . . civilization is multinational, and multilingual (is) . . . spontaneously participated in by a whole series of people . . . (who) . . . may frequently fight among themselves.   Yet they share much the greater part of their civilization, and all the essentials.   A civilization thus is something that has grown up of itself into a supernational product".[3]

Thus, it follows from these different ways of looking at the matter that to define and delimit a civilization in totality not one but several conceptual models are required with such variant frames of reference as the religio-philosophical, the social scientific, the political and aesthetic, along with the depth of culture-history.   But a civilization as a totality, such as the Indian one, is more than just these various ways of analysis because civilizations are organic wholes, and may only be comprehended as such.   Therefore, it is in this organic sense that there is something about India which not only anthropologists are able to characterize as a 'unique configuration', but this organic whole is also evident to the non-academic 'lay'. We may thus say that there is a specific quality of an 'Indianness' of its civilization as opposed to the Chinese or the European ones, etc.   This is very obvious despite the usual contradictory features of India such as in diet, climate, dress, social habits, 'race', religion, etc., of its varied people.   The 'uniqueness' of India is normally, in common parlance, expressed by various words such as 'flavour', 'feel', 'spirit', 'genius', etc., which, for our purpose, do not seem to adequately and precisely express this 'Indian-ness'.   Therefore, the problem now is to first find some appropriate words and concepts which will express and explain the 'uniqueness' of this distinctive cultural tradition and a 'way of life' that suggests a basic consistent unity.   This unity is reflected at various levels and aspects even while it exhibits normal social and cultural change through the passage of time; that is, Indian civilization represents a spatial and temporal continuum in which its carriers come and leave it while it continues on itself, because there are 'certain persistent themes' that dominate the life of the people in this civilization and, thereby, result in a continuum of this distinctiveness of the Indian tradition. Moreover, it is because there is continuity, remembrance and inheritance that one is able to discern an Indian pattern, which has persisted because its institutions for cohesion, order and the maintenance of physical needs are kept up, and not merely because of the oft-repeated spiritual base. One of the most important institutions by which, for example, Indian civilization has largely been, and is, structured is the unique characteristic of its caste system. "While one may find elements of caste like ordering of strata in other societies, there is no other civilization which is itself caste-structured rather than class-structured".[4] Similarly, another of its characteristics is that its participants remember its hoary past through such traditional institutional means as myths, ritual, oral literature, etc.; and that this sacred institutional structure has been transmitted and perpetuated through the characteristic means of the memorization process, and only insignificantly through written literature. In India, memorization has been, and is, a significant and chief means for maintaining continuity in the minds of men.

In any case, the term which seemed most appropriate and expressive for this 'uniqueness' was, Indian Style. "The phrase 'style of life' has come into this discussion to meet the need for a term that will suggest what is most fundamental and enduring about the ways of a group persisting in history. Ethos, basic cultures, patterns, values, configuration of cultures, and modal personality are other terms which have arisen among anthropologists in response to this need".[5] But it should be clarified here that for the maintenance of this 'style of life' the various parts of a civilization do not necessarily have to be uniform. Moreover, the majority of the participants need not also be aware of a pattern of coherence or 'style of life', which is partly a pattern that has been formulated for an understanding by the anthropologist himself.[6] But he also tells us that, today, it is the functional aspect of these institutionalized forms which has integrated the whole of Indian civilization, and has maintained the organizational activity and network of economic, social, cultural (religious) patterns in India. This, in order to facilitate the spread of those cultural, linguistic and religious ideas that "universalize the cultural consciousness of persons within it as they become aware of a greater sphere of common culture".[7]

Thus, it is in terms of understanding the beginnings of the Indian Style that an attempt will be made in this main chapter to interpret some of the early culture-historical data of India which we though might respond fruitfully to such a full-bodied anthropological evaluation. The archaeological evidence that has been chosen for this purpose belongs to what is generally known as the 'proto-historic' period, and it will be viewed in terms of certain cultural and social anthropological concepts, such as by the use of the 'structural-functional' concepts towards the study of society and civilization. The emphasis of this evaluation will be to seek the formative process of Indianization (Indian Style) in terms of the structural and institutional patterns that have persisted until today. But it must also be remembered that this beginning of the Indianization process, or the all-India pattern with which we are concerned here, is only one of the two concrescent processes which characterize the Indian Style. The other equally important process is the differentiation of culture-areas or the regional areas, which may be correlated in the very early stages to the micro-macro 'natural' divisions of the subcontinent. But some aspects of this latter problem will be dealt with later on in the next chapter.

The Indianization problem has not been viewed, it should also be clarified here, in the traditional sense of seeking 'concrete' evidence in terms of any search of 'origins' because the material items of archaeology have been looked at as elements of socio-cultural organization rather than merely as 'concrete data' in the traditional sense. "Language and material goods provide the apparatus whereby social relations are carried on in the community... material objects affect community life in a number of ways... they are the object of property relations, of holdings and transfer; they are the object of emotional attitudes. By their durability, they give manifold links with the past, and so are perpetual conditioning factors to activity..."[8]

Hence, the aim of this chapter is to apply as well as perhaps to ascertain from the specific archaeological evidence certain social scientific (sociological and anthropological) laws and generalizations by means of inductive speculation. It is hoped, thereby, to not only exemplify the integrative inter-disciplinary approach for the study of archaeology but to show that archaeology can also help to contribute towards an understanding of the stability of a 'primary' civilization which has survived into our own century, despite several politico-religious upheavals of later India. Archaeological evidence for the 'protohistoric' period has seldom been viewed in terms of a civilization *in vivo*, i.e., as a cultural whole with respect to characterization of civilization as a 'style' or 'way of life'. There has hardly been any such attempt by either the archaeologist or by the professional student of culture and civilization to evaluate India's early culture-history even though there is an awareness of the almost unique situation of its many millennia long continuity. But if there have been no such attempts, it is because of the use of the old 'shreds and patches' concept of culture which has resulted in India often being called a 'hodge-podge' of a civilization. Similarly, archaeologists, following the old methods of interpretation, have explained away many socio-cultural pheno-mena as if these take place because of purely historical accident, i.e., by means of accidental and at random internal and external relationships. We have earlier noted that the explanations which archaeologists give to their recovered phenomena do not fit in with any currently known dynamics of socio-cultural laws. For instance, some of the problems related to the Harappan civiliza-tion or the Aryan entry into India are explained by the old migration theories as if for the archaeologist almost "the whole course of migration history can be characterized, as a humorous critic put it, as the enterprise of erratic nomads who, with the help of a hygrometer fastened to their saddles, look out to the far horizons to find new pastures in place of those that have sud-denly disappeared".[9] Consequently, it becomes very necessary, before dealing with the archaeological evidence, to give a brief statement of certain key anthropological concepts and definitions which have been utilized by us, in the section below. This is important and useful because the purpose here is of understand-ing the formation, persistence and continuity of the varied socio-cultural elements of early Indian civilization. It should, however, be noted that in illustrating the use of certain anthro-pological definitions and concepts, their controversial nature has not been brought into our discussion because these have been used only as heuristic devices, chiefly for the exemplification of the social science approach to archaeological studies in India.

SOME CONCEPTS FROM ANTHROPOLOGY

Social Anthropology

The following definitions and the associated concepts have been borrowed in a somewhat modified form from A. R. Radcliffe-Brown,[10] who had evolved the concepts of function, process, structure, etc., within a single theory, with reference to the interpretation of human social systems.

Function: The term function has many different meanings in different contexts such as that of logic, mathematics, physiology, organic life, social sciences, etc. In Indian archaeology the concept of function is today not utilized in any current anthropological sense, but its use is merely in a 'utilitarian' sense of whether a tool was used for the purpose of 'cutting', 'sawing', etc. However, it is in the context of human socio-cultural systems that archaeology must define 'function', and in these systems, according to Radcliffe-Brown, "we can recognize the existence of a social structure. Individual human beings, the essential units in this instance, are connected by a definite set of social relations into an integral whole. The continuity of the social structure, like that of an organic structure, is not destroyed by changes in the units. Individuals may leave the society, by death or otherwise, others may enter it. The continuity of structure is maintained by the process of social life, which consists of the activities and interactions of the individual human beings and of the organized groups into which they are united. The social life of the community is here defined as the *functioning* of the social structure. The *function* of any recurrent activity, such as the punishment of a crime, or a funeral ceremony, is the part it plays in the social life as a whole and therefore the contribution it makes to the maintenance of the structural continuity.

"The concept of function as here defined involves the notion of a *structure* consisting of a *set of relations* amongst unit *entities*, the *continuity* of the structure being maintained by a *life process* made up of the *activities* of the constituent units... Such a view implies that a social system has a certain kind of unity, which we may speak of as a fundamental unity. We may define it with a sufficient degree of harmony or internal consistency, i.e., without producing persistent conflicts which can neither be resolved nor regulated".[11]

Process: The above-stated functional approach may convey to the reader the meaning that a given society or civilization remains static in a state of equilibrium and that any kind of change in the set-up implies a break in continuity. But this is not the case because what is also implicit in this concept (at any rate, as I would like it to be understood) is that structures are adaptive, and adaptation itself is a *process*. Thus, although human societies function within socio-cultural systems and have an inner structure yet they are also in a state of change. However, opposed to this view are certain old concepts of a 'static' state of a given society such as, for instance, the Harappan one that has often been called a 'stagnant' society, and within which most of the changes have invariably been derived from 'external' sources. But even recent archaeological evidence, apart from any reliance on socio-cultural laws of human society, clearly suggests that change was inherent in Harappan society as is seen, for example, at Lothal where there were "two standards of weights and more than three sizes of bricks. The widths of the streets and the sizes of the houses varied greatly".[12]

At any rate, the 'structural-functional' approach does not conflict with the concept of process and change, because change is inherent not only in all human societies but in nature itself. Thus, the best approach for archaeology seems to be a dual one; that is, research in archaeology at the synchronic and diachronic levels is essential for an understanding of archaeological phenomena in any meaningful way. "A study of ancestry from a functional point of view leads to fuller understanding of the function, and of course a study of function from the point of view of ancestry helps in an understanding of the ancestry".[13]

The following is how Radcliffe-Brown has defined social and cultural process: ". . . the concrete reality with which the social anthropologist is concerned is not any sort of entity but a process... The unit of investigation is some particular region of the earth during a certain period of time. The process itself consists of an immense multitude of actions and interactions of human beings, acting as individuals or in combination of groups. Amidst the diversity of the particular events there are discoverable regularities... In a particular society one can discover certain process of *cultural tradition*, using the word tradition, in its literal meaning of handing on or handing down... If we treat the social reality that we are investigating as being not an entity but a process, then culture and cultural tradition are names for certain recognizable aspects of that process... The transmission of learnt ways of thinking, feeling and acting constitutes the cultural process, which is a specific feature of human social life. It is, of course, part of that process of interaction amongst persons which is here defined as the social process, thought of as social reality".[14]

Structure: Radcliffe-Brown has explained social structure in terms of some sort of ordered arrangement of its parts or components in which the units "are *persons*, and a person is a human being considered not as an organism but as occupying position in a social structure... One of the fundamental theoretical problems of sociology is that of the nature of social continuity. Continuity in the form of social life depends upon structural continuity, that is, some sort of continuity in the arrangements of persons in relation to one another... A nation, a tribe, a clan, a body... can continue in existence as an arrangement of persons though the personnel, the units of which each is composed, changes from time to time. There is continuity of the structure, just as the human body, of which the components are molecules, preserves a continuity of structure though the actual molecules, of which the body consists, are continually changing... but the structure as an arrangement remains continuous... The social relationships, of which the continuing network constitute social structure, are not haphazard conjunctions of individuals but are determined by the social process and any relationship is one in which the conduct of persons in their interactions with each other is controlled by norms, rules or patterns. . ."[15]

Institution: The "established norms of conduct of a particular form of social life, it is usual to refer to an institution. . . The institutions refer to a distinguishable type or class of social relationships and interactions. . . Thus an institution may be said to have its *raison d'être* (sociological origin) and its particular *raison d'être* (historical origin). The first is for the sociologist or social anthropologist to discover by the comparative method. The second is for the historian to discover by examination of records or for the ethnologist . . . in the absence of records, to speculate about. . ."[16]

Organization: "The concept is clearly closely related to the concept of social structure, but it is desirable not to treat the two terms as synonymous. A convenient use, which does not depart from common usage in English, is to define social structure as an arrangement of persons in institutionally controlled or defined relationship. . . We may say that when we are dealing with a structural system we are concerned with a system of social *positions*, while in an organization we deal with a system of roles".[17]

System: Radcliffe-Brown has viewed human society as a system with reference to the problem of their persistence, and defines a system as a set of relations between a set of entities. But these relations do not remain unchanged, i.e., there is not only static continuity but that there is a dynamic continuity, whereby a society retains its structural form during a certain period of time even though it may lose certain other obvious characteristic forms as tangible material items, persons, etc.[18] "Society is a system in the sense, that in any description we could make of the society, or of what constitutes the culture, all characteristics to greater or lesser extent function together consistently. The degree of consistency varies from society to society... A social system anywhere in the world will continue only on certain conditions, and one of these is the maintenance of a particular body of cosmological beliefs. On these beliefs hangs the whole social structure of a society. Destroy these beliefs and you destroy the whole structure".[19] This concept of system may well be applied within the framework of structure, function and process, to the evidence of the well-known Harappan society. Thus, for instance, there may be seen an obvious internal consistency in the structuring of Harappan society which had persisted for several hundreds of years because the parts of the structure, the system, including the cosmological characteristic of that society had probably worked together to reinforce each other and maintain the structure.[20]

Cultural Anthropology

There have been many attempts, as has been stated, to understand the beginnings of Indian civilization, but these have generally been carried out in a descriptive manner, in vague and undefined terms of comprehension rather than within any precise words, terms and concepts of anthropology (social sciences). Therefore, the problem for us is of how, now, to envisage the beginnings, persistence and continuity of this unique 'configuration' called Indian civilization, in terms of certain systems, structure, and organizational institutions which have enabled its style to survive. In this context, we found that the concepts of culture and civilization as enunciated by the late Robert Redfield seem to give the best frame of reference for the archaeological evidence at hand. His approach, of course, has been applied to certain contemporary village studies in various parts of the world, including India. But our concern here is not with his 'micro-level' frame of reference. It is, instead, with the 'macro-level' of Redfield's approach to the study of larger 'societal wholes' called civilizations. But in applying these concepts to the evidence of archaeology, the task is complex and difficult because of the incomplete nature of the evidence which is not easily amenable to the kind of analysis that the social scientist has at his disposal. Nevertheless, the concepts of Robert Redfield were found very useful for our attempt to understand the beginnings of the Indian Style, and it is worth noting the following statement of his with regard to the 'primary' civilizations of India and China: ". . . where civilization is indigenous, having developed out of the precivilized people of that very culture, converting them into the peasant half of the same culture-civilization . . . (the) . . . continuity with their own native civilization has persisted. Chinese and Indian peasants remain connected with their own native civilizations . . . (the). . . peasant tradition affects the doctrine of the learned . . . (and) . . . constitutes the social structure of culture, the structure of tradition. From this point of view a civilization is an organization of specialists, of kinds of role occupiers in characteristic functions concerned with the transmission of tradition . . . the investigator sees a small society that is not an isolate, that is not complete in itself, that bears not only a side-by-side relation but also an up-and-down relation to the folk and tribal peoples, on the one hand, and to towns and cities, on the other. In some places the two-way relationship is both logical and actual. . ."[21] (Fig. 1).

We thus note that, specifically for India, the common experience of this 'intuitive' whole, of something recognized as complex but taken as one thing, has been very aptly stated by Redfield in more formal terms.[22] This unique character has been explained by him as another system in which the internal interrelationships are understandable because there is an arrangement of its related part. He sees ". . . civilization as kinds of ways of life in relationships both persisting and yet changing, with one another. India has long had towns and cities, peasants and primitive or tribal communities. These

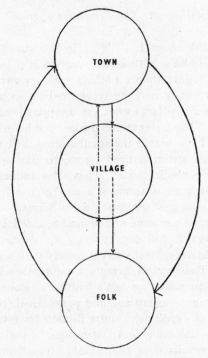

Fig. 1. Folk-Peasant-Urban Interaction

kinds of subsidiary societies and cultures are enduring, as types or classes . . . the peasant there . . . (are) . . . one of the kinds of people recognized in that civilization as occupying a characteristic position, in function and status. I can think of the inner structure of Indian civilization as spatial, as it were, mechanical or organic interrelation of such kinds of people. Then I will see some of the things going on in India. If I use some such idea, however suggestive and undeclared, the immense number and variety of facts about India fall into some arrangements. . .

I began to think about India".[23]   He also states that the long
continuity of India's culture-history gives it a personality that
is positively distinct from all others with its own story to tell,
and that this entity may be recognized as such by its participants of which the large numbers comprise peasants and folk
communities.   The latter communities may be involved in their
daily round of life within the small cosmos, but their activities
lead them, in institutionalized forms, to deal with the urban
aspect of their civilization.[24]   Thus, the Indian villager and
even the tribal man is as much a part of the Indian Style or
'way of life' as is the 'sophisticated' urbanite.

The following are some of the modified definitions:

Folk-Society: A folk-society may be ˉdefined as a small,
isolated, non-literate, homogeneous society with a strong sense of
solidarity.   "The ways of living are conventionalized into that
coherent system which we call a 'culture'.   Behaviour is traditional, spontaneous, uncritical, and personal: there is no legisla-
tion or habit of experiment and reflection for intellectual ends.
Kinship, its relationship and institutions, is the unit of action.
The sacred prevails over the secular; the economy is one of
status rather than of the market".[25]   The economy of folk-
societies is a self-sufficient one and it differs from truly 'primitive' hunting and gathering societies in that the folk-societies
have contact with centres of intellectual thought and development, i.e., with civilization.   However, according to another
author, the terms "Folk culture and folk society are not inter-
changeable as the former may be thought of as a common way
of life which characterizes some or all of the people of many
villages, towns and cities within a given area. . .   A folk
society may be thought of as organized groups of individuals
characterized by a folk culture".[26]

Peasant Society: The description of peasants by Redfield,
following Eric Wolf, is that "their agriculture is a livelihood
and a way of life, not a business for profits . . . the peasant is a

man who is in effective control of a piece of land to which he has long been attached by ties of tradition and sentiment. The same fields are cultivated year after year, and new land comes into cultivation only slowly: for the most part people go on living in the same houses and cultivating the same land from year to year. The land and he are parts of one thing, one old-tested body of relationships".[27] In the context of Indian civilization, he continues, "peasants are the rural dimension who control and cultivate their land for subsistence and as a part of a traditional way of life who look to and are influenced by gentry or towns people whose way of life is like theirs but in a more civilized form".[28]

Urban Society: The meaning of the urban concept is well known. But quite often there is a confusion in the use of a word like city because a distinction is seldom made between the industrial and pre-industrial city. It is only the pre-industrial urban communities which are relevant for the present, i.e., those communities which have arisen without stimulus from that form of production which one associates with the European industrial revolution. There is, therefore, a certain closeness of the pre-industrial urban areas and the countryside peasants. In fact, the peasants and the pre-industrial urban areas are an integral part of a pre-industrial civilization.

"Pre-industrial cities depend for their existence upon food and raw material obtained from without, for this reason they are marketing centres. And they serve as centres for handicraft manufacturing. In addition, they fulfil important 'political', religious and educational functions . . . The proportion of urbanites relative to the peasant population is small. . . The economic system of the pre-industrial city, based as it has been upon animal sources of power, articulates with a characteristic class structure and family . . . of class structure, the most striking component is a literate elite controlling and depending for its existence upon the mass of its populace. . . The member of the elite belong to the 'correct' families and enjoy power, property, and certain highly valued personal attributes. Their position, moreover, is legitimatized by sacred writings".[29]

In the pre-industrial context of peasant-urban relationship, "a market means both a state of mind and a place to trade . . . the field is not spatially defined; it is a set of activities, attitudes, and relationships that belong together wherever and whenever. . . One can also describe the people who move about the country from one market, in the former sense, to another town market. Taken together, these ambulatory merchants in all their relationships of trade are another kind of market with definition upon the land . . . (these are) described the regions in which goods of one kind or another are sold, and the regions from which (are) drawn buyers who come to centres of sale and distribution (such as) markets, centering on crossroads, fairs . . . it is the social field . . . network of relationship of all kinds of the rural people with one another . . . let us call it the country-wide network . . . and we find village tied to village . . . and town to countryside, in a web of social relations. . . This is what we do find in India . . . each local community connected with many other local communities through caste. The internal unity of the village is qualified or balanced by the unity that is felt by the villager with a fellow caste member of another village. In the cases of the higher castes this unity may be felt over wide areas, and it may be institutionalized by genealogists and caste historians. . . Furthermore, country-wide network or rural relationship . . . (is) widespread through connections of marriage.

"In short, the principal elements of the country-wide network of India consist in familial and caste associations that persist through generations. These associations connect one set of villages with another or some of the families in one village with families corresponding in culture and social status in other villages. It is as if the characteristic social structure of the primitive self-contained community had been dissected out and its components spread about a wide area. Rural India is a primitive or a tribal society rearranged to fit a civilization. . . Yet the local differences within the great civilizations have to be recognized. . ."[30]

Great and Little Tradition: In addition to the folk-urban concept stated above, there is also Redfield's well-known concept of the Great and Little Tradition. This is with reference to his attempt to understand the structure of Indian tradition, and is also known by such other terms as the 'high and low', 'folk and classic', 'popular and learned', and the 'hierarchic and lay'. The two traditions are interdependent, according to Redfield, and have long affected each other and continue to do so. "Great and little tradition can be thought of as two currents of thought and action, distinguishable, yet ever flowing into and out of each other. . . The great tradition is cultivated in schools or temples; the little tradition works itself out and keeps itself going in the lives of the unlettered in their village communities. . . If we enter a village within a civilization we see at once that the culture there has been flowing into it from teachers and exemplars who never saw that village, who did their work in intellectual circles far away in space and time. . ."[31]

In other words, in India, at the very top may be placed the philosophical developments formulated by the great religious leaders, and lower down the scale of hierarchy may be placed the myths, ritual, lower gods, etc. It is also seen that in the 'Hindu' tradition of India the main works of Brahmanism have throughout history incorporated within them the 'lower' myths, gods, etc., which are presented in these religious treatises as unified cycles of stories within a well-formulated and sophisticated framework. On the other hand, in a similar process, peasant castes may often bear the same name as some aboriginal tribe in the same region; or in the country festivals may be noticed that many of the cults and rituals are of primitive tribal origin even though the actual tribe may have vanished. Therefore, since times immemorial the literate tradition of 'Hinduism' has adopted and readjusteu many of the 'lower' gods into its own tradition, just as the peasants and tribals have adopted and taken the 'higher' gods and rituals within their own socio-economic framework (Fig. 2). But it must be remembered that this interaction of the 'higher' and 'lower' tradition is yet another instance of one of the institutionalized forms which maintains the cultural unity or Style of India, along with the other unifying institutions of caste, familial systems, trade relations, etc. These various institutions have maintained the structural unity of Indian civilization, enforced by the interrelatedness of village, folk and urban society.

Thus, to conclude this section, what is being suggested is that, if following this 'structural-functional' approach one looks at the early culture-historical period of India, the various facts of archaeological evidence begin to fall into a meaningful pattern. It is by means of this view that it is possible to trace the five millennia long thread of continuity in the Indian socio-cultural and socio-economic realm, i.e., if we look at the evidence of the exchange of ceramic styles and forms and other material items of archaeology as elements of socio-cultural organization. Similarly, we will also have to view within the socio-cultural context the various 'survivals' that may be discerned within the present make-up of the complex Indian civilization, such as the various elements of the 'primitive' tribal and folk-cultures as well as the 'pre-Aryan' Harappan survivals and other non-Aryan 'cultures'. That is, along with the 'survival' of these myths, beliefs, and other material items, etc., there are generally also present corresponding socio-cultural institutions which enable the large number of various elements to survive. The fairly simple reason behind this statement is that all these 'survivals' in 'tangible' or 'intangible' forms are often related to the socio-economic system which, in turn, is interrelated to the socio-cultural system. Thus, if perchance the basic socio-economic

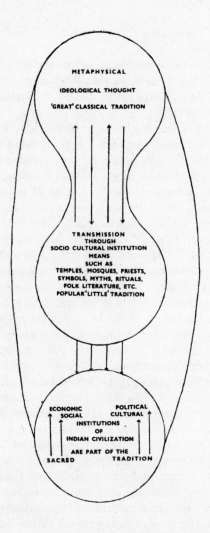

Fig. 2. Great and Little Tradition

and socio-cultural structure of Indian society had not remained the same, then very few 'survivals' would have been discernible today, and there would also have been a lack of continuity in Indian civilization.

At any rate, this is the basic framework of the present approach which should be taken up as no more than a heuristic device. Therefore, as there is theoretical progress in both anthropology and archaeology, this approach may involve further clarifications, refinements and addition of important variables, etc., or perhaps this framework may even be rejected for a more suitable one. Hence, whether the models and definitions employed here will be valid for other schemes and problems is not the main issue. *The main aim here is to lay stress on the need to utilize some socio-cultural frames of reference within which archaeological evidence should be viewed*, such as has been applied in the section below to understand the Formative Period of Indian civilization. This has been carried out as far as it was possible to do so with the available archaeological evidence, perhaps at the risk of exaggerating our approach. But as this is not a descriptive monograph of 'facts', a great deal of archaeological facts will naturally be left unsaid because in order to "illustrate a principle you must exaggerate much and you must omit much".[32] Nevertheless, it is hoped that this exaggeration will be balanced by bringing into prominence certain different aspects to the study of Indian archaeology which have thus far been neglected by the traditional approach. In this manner it is hoped that Indian archaeology will also be able to contribute to certain recent studies of contemporary Indian civilization and society which are being carried out by anthropologists. These studies, however, require support from culture-history for giving the long-range perspective which the anthropologist himself is well aware of such as Marriott who, for instance, says, "Up to this point I have indicated only some very recent evidence for the interaction of village structure and state government...

Yet if such interaction is evident in 1952, in 1882, or 1822, it may also have been occurring for centuries, even for millenniums, in the past... But exclusive use of such short-run perspectives is likely to carry with it the misleading implications that before the heterogenic influences of recent times villages were somehow isolated and free..."[33]

ARCHAEOLOGICAL EVIDENCE

The term Formative Period that has been used in this monograph, instead of the 'proto-historic' period, is not in the sense as it is used in the archaeology of the New World. But it has been used in the general sense as has been defined by the Braidwoods.[34] This general definition formulated by them is an elaboration of the three eras of Julian Steward's scheme. But in the modified definition suited for the Indian subcontinent, this period may be identified in its earlier stages by the presence of self-sufficient 'folk' communities and, later on, by the presence of certain basic technologies among the peasant cultures when craft specialization (including incipient metallurgy) had already begun. There may now be seen the beginnings of trade, regional 'cultural' variation, the expansion of settlements in inter-riverine areas, and the beginnings of towns, temples, markets, etc.

Thus, in terms of this definition, the following is an account of the Indian Formative Period, supported by C_{14} dates[35] (Fig. 3). This is specially as it emerges from the results of the important explored and excavated sites of the main peasant-urban Harappan system during the third millennium B.C. and of the remaining peasant and folk spheres in the second millennium B.C. In this picture (Fig. 4) each interacting sphere with its associated cultural items, ceramic styles, forms and shapes, etc., has 'cultural' affiliations with the other spheres. This, in archaeological terms, is chiefly reflected by the diagnostic trait lists and other items. These spheres also seem to more or less

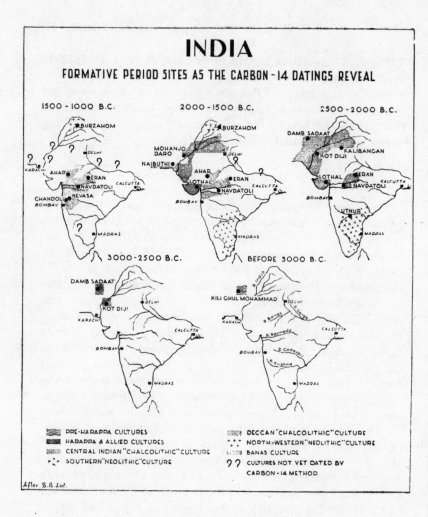

Fig. 3. The Formative Period as the C_{14} Datings Reveal

coincide with the 'natural' regions, suggesting that these spheres are important from the cultural-ecological viewpoint. But this problem will be dealt with in the next chapter.

The following are the main spheres and the important sites within each of them:

A. The peasant-urban spheres of the Harappan (early and late) and allied sites.

   (i) Baluchistan region includes such sites as Rana-Gundai, Periano-Gundai, Moghul-Gundai, Togau, Kulli, Mehi, Londo and Kili Gul Mohammed, etc.

  (ii) Indus region includes such sites as Amri, Nal, Kot-Diji, Mohenjodaro, Harappa, Chanhudaro, etc.

 (iii) Rajasthan region includes such sites as Kalibangan, Tekkwada, Chak-86, etc.

 (iv) Trans-Gangetic Plain includes such sites as Rupar, Bara, etc.

  (v) Upper Gangetic Plain includes the important site of Alamgirpur, some 28 miles north-east of Delhi.

 (vi) Gujarat region (including Kathiawad) includes such sites as Rangpur, Lothal, Prabhas, Rojdi, Bhagatrav, etc.

B. The peasant sphere of 'Central Indian chalcolithic' sites.

   (i) North-Central Hills region includes such sites as Navdatoli, Maheshwar, Eran, etc.

C. The peasant sphere of 'Banas chalcolithic' sites.

   (i) The North-West Hills region includes such sites as Ahar, Gilund, Nagda, Ujjain, etc.

D. The peasant sphere of 'Deccan chalcolithic' sites.

   (i) The North Deccan region includes such sites as Nevasa, Bahal, Prakash, Nasik, Jorwe, Daimabad, Chandoli, etc.

E. The folk sphere of the 'Southern stone-celt neolithic'.

   (i) The South Deccan region includes such sites as Piklihal, Utnur, Sangankallu, Brahmagiri, Narsipur, Nagarjunakonda, etc.

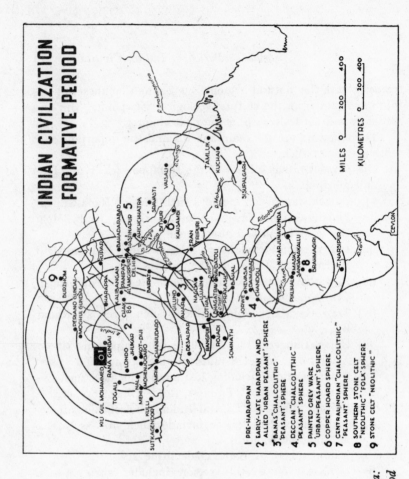

Fig. 4.
Civilization in India:
The Formative Period

F. The folk sphere of the 'Northern stone-celt neolithic'.
   (i) Kashmir region includes the very crucial site of Burzahom.
G. The 'Painted Grey-ware' area of such sites as Ahichchhatrā,
   Śrāvastī, Kauśāmbī, Tamluk, Vaiśālī, Sisupalgarh, etc.

Besides these main spheres where one is on surer archaeologi-
cal grounds, there are the following areas in Eastern India in
which the archaeological details are not very clear:
H. The 'Copper Hoard' area of such sites as Bithur, Bahadura-
   bad, etc.
I. The 'chalcolithic' area of sites in Bihar, Orissa and West
   Bengal.
J. The 'Eastern square shouldered stone-celt neolithic' sites in
   Assam, and adjoining areas.

In the above briefly enumerated archaeological picture of
the interacting spheres during the Formative Period, the most
important sphere is the peasant-urban one of the Harappan and
allied sites. The details for the various cultures in the different
spheres are known in archaeological literature, specially about
the Harappan civilization which has been made quite well known
by the writings of Marshall,[36] Mackay,[37] Piggot,[38] Childe,[39]
Wheeler,[40] etc. But it is essential to give some of the salient
features of the Harappan society and culture in order to
illustrate our viewpoint, as follows.

The known Harappan urban areas were elaborately planned
and executed, and were composed of buildings with one or more
storeys as well as small tenements and large houses, etc. All
these buildings were made from both sun-dried and kiln-burnt
bricks. The planning of the urban area was based on the grid
pattern, i.e., there were broad and narrow streets and lanes which
cut each other at right angles, and the town was provided with
an underground system of pipes and drains for rain and sewage
purposes. There were also public and private baths (but no
W.C.'s), market-places, granaries, etc. The urban areas were

generally dominated by a walled acropolis which was probably the residence of 'authority', and upon which were also places of assembly.   The 'acropolis' was protected by flood embankments, defence fortifications, etc.   The granaries present in the Harappan urban areas had most probably formed the economic focus, and were under the control of an 'agency' which may also have been the 'authority' that 'ruled'.   But more of these and other inferences came later on.

Cuneiform texts of Old Babylonia and other evidence suggest that trade was carried along the 800 miles of coastlines.   The site of Lothal in Gujarat, with its probable dockyard, also exemplifies this maritime trade.   These texts tell us, for example, that Ur was the principal port of entry into Mesopotamia at the time of the dynasty of Larsa.   At Ur, an inscribed tablet mentions various items which the sailors, probably coming from the Harappan civilization, offer to the goddess Ningal.[41]   The offerings mentioned in these inscriptions include gold, silver, copper, lapis lazuli, stone beads, ivory combs and inlays, eye-paints, certain wooden objects, etc.   But in addition to this Harappan trade with the West Asians, there is also inferential evidence of 'trade' and exploitation which extended inland into further India, eastwards and southwards.   This is indicated by our knowledge of the identification and location of the raw materials which were, most probably, exploited for the needs of the Harappan socio-economic system.   The nearest sources for the exploitation of the raw materials which the Harappan and allied communities may have utilized (thereby creating culture-contact situations within the subcontinent) are as follows:

Copper is found in Baluchistan, Rajputana, South India and Afghanistan; *tin* in Bengal and Afghanistan; *silver* sources are in Ajmer and South India; *lapis lazuli* sources are only in Badakshan in north-east Afghanistan; *gold* sources are in Mysore and Kandhar; *turquoise* could have come from the Pamirs, Kashmir, Persia, Tibet or Burma; *jade* is found only in Mysore;

the nearest source for *amazonite* is in Hirapura, Gujarat; and *marble* sources are in Rajputana.[42]

This suggests an extensive search for the exploitation of raw materials, and it clearly implies 'professional' trading classes, at least of some sort, who could have only functioned within certain institutionalized forms of behaviour, specially whenever these 'expeditions' came into contact with other cultural groups in whose regions these raw materials existed. It should be remembered that the subcontinent outside the Harappan sphere was not *terra incognita*. Therefore, implicit also in these situations of 'trade' and of 'exchange' is not only the continuity in the maintenance of some form of the old 'trading posts' but also of the establishment of new settlements, etc., with the expansion of exploitation, 'exchange' and 'trade'. The discovery of new sites in recent years outside the Indus region tends to support this view, and these discoveries have necessitated a radical reappraisal of the old views about that civilization.

The extensions of the Harappa civilization have now been located eastwards into East Panjab, U.P., North Rajputana, Bikaner and southwards all over Saurashtra and southern Gujarat as far as at least Surat which is only 175 miles north of Bombay. Some of these regional sites such as Kalibangan and Lothal which have been horizontally excavated are replicas of the Indus urban areas, albeit with their regional variation that is reflected in the ceramic designs, forms and fabrics as well as in the absence of one or the other typical Harappan features. But both the old and new urban sites show remarkable uniformity in town-planning, sanitation, pottery, seals, ornaments, weights and measures, funerary customs, etc.[43] Some of the other Harappan sites which are outside of the Indus region are contemporaneous with the early Harappan sites of the main valley, while some others are later and continued to exist in one form or the other long after the large cities had 'vanished' from the Indus basin. Sites in Gujarat, such as Rangpur and Lothal, and to some extent at Bara and Rupar in East Panjab, indicate that in the late Harappan levels the older cultural traits were replaced very gradually and not suddenly as was the case in the main valley. For instance, the *level IIb* of Rangpur, which is equivalent to *level B* of Lothal, is a transitional phase that is characterized by new elements and forms of pottery, such as small blades and lustrous-red-ware, etc.[44] (Fig. 5). These new elements finally emerge in *Rangpur III*. Similarly, sites of the late Harappan variety and the so-called 'degenerate' post-Harappan 'survival' sites seem to have continued in Kathiawad, at such sites as Prabhas, Rojdi, etc.[45]

In other words, without getting into further discussion of the archaeological details, the discovery of the new sites suggests very strongly that the peasant-urban Harappan sphere was spreading, with regional and local variations, to the east and south of the Indus basin. But before discussing the socio-cultural implications of the Harappan civilization and its spread, the archaeological evidence of the interlocking of sites within and without the Harappan sphere will be given below. It should be borne in mind, to repeat, that the archaeological evidence of the traits and elements in this interlocking has been viewed within the 'total' socio-cultural and socio-economic contexts, and not merely by the old concepts which explain archaeological items and traits in terms only of diffusion, accidental exchanges, survivals, independent inventions, etc.

1. *Archaeological evidence of culture-contact situations within the Harappan peasant-urban sphere*

(a) The culture-contact situations between the various sites, as evidenced in the ceramic forms and designs, etc. seem to have already begun in the pre-Harappan levels as, for instance, during the time of what has been called the "substratum of the Sothi elements".[46] These pre-Harappan elements persist and

continue into the level of the 'mature Harappan' in the Baluchistan and the Indus Valley sites,[47] as well as at the newer Harappan sites of Kalibangan and Rupai. Similarly, at Kot-Diji, there are present 'defence' and foundation structures made of stone in the pre-Harappan levels. This technique of using stone material also continues in the main Harappan levels. These spatial and temporal culture-contacts and continuities that are seen during the pre-Harappan times continue into the main Harappan levels, and must also have a "bearing on the genesis of the Harappa civilization".[48]

(b) There are the other culture-contact situations which are seen between the Harappan sites in the Indus Valley and those towards the western periphery in Baluchistan as, for instance, between Mohenjodaro and the sites of Kulli, Ghazi Shah, Pandiwahi, Pai-jo-Kotiro.[49] Once again, these contact situations are reflected mainly in the Harappan ceramic forms and motifs. But it is also important to note the close identity of Suktagen-Dor with Desalpar, in terms of the technique of building similar stone-walls and streets, etc.[50]

(c) Culture-contacts of the Indus Valley Harappan sites is seen in such items as seals, pottery, etc., with sites to its south and east, such as with those of Lothal, Alamgirpur, Rupar and others. This is quite well known and needs no repetition here. But this close cultural identity should be looked at in terms of the spread and expansion of certain common socio-cultural and socio-economic Harappan systems and ideas rather than by any 'colonization' in terms of a large-scale population movement, which explanation is normally suggested. This cultural identity implies, instead, a process of the incorporation of indigenous non-Harappan societies into the Harappan peasant-urban system. It is also supported by the fact that there is a continuity, from the Formative Period until today, of the population composition of the known 'physical' human types that are found in the regions of Sind, Panjab and Gujarat.[51]

2. *Archaeological evidence of culture-contact situations between the Harappan peasant-urban sphere and the other non-Harappan spheres, within the subcontinent*

We have already mentioned some of the reasons for the establishment of contacts within India, such as the need for the exploitation of raw materials which was important for both internal 'consumption' and external trade, and it could only have taken place within certain established socio-cultural and socio-economic rules and norms. But some support for these inferences may also be given by the *meagre* evidence from archaeology. This is as follows:

(a) There is evidence of close cultural affiliations between Lothal, Rangpur and Desalpar, with the sites of 'Banas culture',[52] in the evidences of the Black and Red ceramic wares.

(b) It has been suggested that one of the anthropomorphic figures found at some of the 'Copper Hoard' sites of the Gangetic Valley is similar to the one which was found in the Late Harappan levels at Lothal.[53]

(ci) At Bahadurabad, which is an 'Ochre-coloured-pottery' (O.C.P.) ware site, the presence of the short-stemmed dish-on-stand and the extensively incised ware, etc. suggests not only temporal continuity of certain ceramic types but, most probably, also contemporary cultural contacts with the Harappans.[54]

(cii) It has been suggested that there is a great similarity in fabric, shape, etc. of the O.C.P. ware which is found at Atranjikhera, Manpura, Bhatpura, Ambkheri, etc., with those of the Harappan wares that are found at Rupar, Bara, etc.[55]

(ciii) At Bargaon, limited excavations have revealed typical Harappan pottery with black painted designs on a red surface, as well as the chevron decoration on a ring stone. These designs and decorations show remote inspiration from Kalibangan.[56] At Bargaon, there are also present certain other pottery shapes and paintings which suggest contacts with Cemetery 'H', and this again is the case at Ambkheri.[57] A copper ring was found at Bargaon and Ambkheri among a typical Harappan style assemblage, and this ring is of the same type as was reported from Pondi, Bahadurabad and Jorwe. This "calls for fresh thinking as regards the relationship of the Harappan with the so-called O.C.P."[58]

(d) The evidence at the site of Atranjikhera indicates cultural affinities, in terms of the Black and Red ware group, with similar wares found at Lothal and Rangpur. Moreover, the C_{14} dates of the lowest Black and Red ware levels at Atranjikhera also suggest contemporaneity with the late Harappan levels.[59]

(e) In the late levels of many of the 'proto-historic' sites in Saurashtra there is evidence of the presence of the regional variation of some of the Harappan ceramic styles. These 'stylistic' elements are also seen at certain sites in the regions around Ahar and Gilund, in the Udaipur and Chitorgarh districts of Rajasthan.[60]

(f) The evidence from a site, which unfortunately is now drowned in a dammed lake on the Chambal river, in the Mandasaur district of Madhya Pradesh, was very interesting. This site had indicated that prior to the appearance of the 'Malwa Chalcolithic', there was present a pottery which was akin to the pottery both from Ahar and Harappa. It has been claimed that this lost site had very significantly revealed some other familiar urban Harappan traits, such as raised platforms, city defence walls, etc.[61]

3.   *Archaeological evidence of culture-contact situations amongst the other non-Harappan spheres*

(a) At Kallur, in the Raichur district of Andhra Pradesh, were found antennae swords that were most probably made locally but which also show a great similarity to the Fategarh swords of the Gangetic plains.   It has similarly been suggested that the Kallur swords were imported from the Eastern zone.[62]

(b) The evidence of the copper celts from Navadatoli,[63] the antennae dagger of Chandoli,[64] a dagger with midrib at Nevasa,[65] and probably the broken copper man found in the upper levels of Lothal,[66] all these show affinities to similar objects and types that were found at the various 'Copper Hoard' sites.

(c) The full-fledged peasant sites of Central and Western India show clear interrelations with such far-away regions as Iran in types and forms of their ceramic wares,[67] along with the widespread use of the West Asian 'Crested-guiding technique'.[68]

(d) There are distinct culture-contact situations to be seen between the 'chalcolithic' cultures of Malwa and Maharashtra with those of the 'neolithic' ones of Andhra and Karnatak, and this forms the interaction network of the 'neolithic' and the 'chalcolithic' spheres.   For instance, in the upper strata of such typical 'neolithic' sites as Piklihal, Brahmagiri and Maski, there is the occurrence of copper which suggests contacts with sites of the 'chalcolithic' sphere of the Northern Deccan.[69]   It may, once again, be noted that the population composition of the 'physical' types in these two interaction spheres continues to be the same in these regions even today,[70] as it was during those times.

(e) The typical South Indian stone-celt type with an elliptical section is also found at some sites in Eastern India, together with the characteristic square-shouldered stone-celt of the region.[71]

(f) The Northern 'neolithic' site of Burzahom in Kashmir shows 'cultural' affinities with the rest of India because 'neolithic' stone-celts and a fragmentary ringstone that were found in the Kangra district have been correlated to both the Kashmir and the South Indian 'neolithic' types.[72]   These Northern 'neolithic' types had, previously, also been found near Harappa and Attock in the Indus Valley.[73]

(g) On the other hand, the evidence of the harvester and the pit-dwellings from Burzahom also show contacts with similar types from the Neolithic Period of China and Japan, and are familiar traits that are also to be found in the Far East.[74]

Thus, it may be concluded from the brief survey stated above that all these material evidences of culture-contact situations which are to be seen in the records of archaeology necessarily imply the establishment of some 'institutionalized' forms of socio-cultural and socio-economic behaviour, even if it was for purposes of distant exploitation of raw materials or for exchange and trade in finished products such as ceramic wares, metal tools, beads made of sea-shells, etc., which the peasant communities may have required. The presence of even rare metal tools suggests that such culture-contacts were perhaps maintained by means of roaming 'ambulatory traders', and the presence of metal tools itself implies craft specialization and the development of trade and other socio-economic relationships.

At any rate, there is clear evidence by the middle of the second millennium B.C. for the increased frequency of these culture-contact situations between the various interacting spheres. All this results, when viewed within the broad socio-cultural context, in the formation of the indigenous 'primary' Indian civilization, the beginnings of which had already been made, at least, a thousand years earlier. But by now, these contacts were even more well established into institutionalized forms because, to repeat, all these various contacts in any form do not take place at random and in a 'vacuum', as one learns from the socio-anthropological laws and generalizations. The interaction of the various spheres also implies that gradually there developed a closeness of the urban and village craftsmen (through perhaps many kinds of personal and impersonal and formal varieties of socio-cultural relations) who now, probably, formed distinct social classes, occupational specialists, etc. This spread of the peasant-urban social organization, in which specialists are present, implies stricter social control, marriage rules and regulations, etc. But these other inferences of a socio-cultural nature will be dealt with in the next section.

In any case, the Indian subcontinent by the end of the second millennium B.C. was inhabited by the various interacting 'cultures' which were spread all over. By the end of the first millennium B.C. such interlocking and overlaps of archaeological evidence are very clear and quite evident, and the subcontinent up to the borders of Mysore was inhabited, and these various kinds of socio-cultural and socio-economic relationships were well established. By the time of iron technology, attempt at the political spread and unification by various 'kingdoms' was on its way.

SOCIO-CULTURAL INFERENCES OF SOME HARAPPAN EVIDENCE

The historically-oriented concepts which until now have been utilized to understand the Harappan evidence are based on rather simplified old theories and explanations, through the use of borrowed expressive terms from art, literature, psychology, etc., which have certainly given romance and illumination to this ancient civilization. However, even where any such generalizations may be justified, the frames of reference utilized have provided a rather poor fit to the data, and have also not given any great incentive for furthering fundamental archaeological research. Moreover, by not utilizing the far-reaching developments in the social sciences, the loss of information that has resulted in such simplified explanations has been great. It is against this re-evaluative background of the rejection of many of the previous general interpretations and explanations, therefore, that the archaeological evidence of the Harappa civilization (and society) will now be freshly examined. However, for the present, it is only possible to discuss some of the major problems related to this society, specially to illustrate that the problem-oriented approach to the study of archaeology will yield greater socio-cultural information than has been hitherto possible.

A. *Some problems related to the subsistence-economic base of Harappan society*

It is generally accepted that the huge granaries in the Harappan urban areas had probably formed the economic focus because these granaries reflect the apparent surplus on which the urban non-agricultural population was fed and maintained. But what exactly the implications of 'surplus' are, has never been questioned or discussed, since both the archaeologists and the anthropologists have implicitly accepted the surplus theory that was specially developed by Childe, following Marx, in his 'Urban Revolution'[75] and other works. The argument developed by Childe was that social stratification (class-specialization) and the increase in population had become possible only because of the increased quantity of abundant food 'surplus' which had enabled the release of greater leisure time. However, food 'surplus' in any given society, whether it is persuaded or compelled, is determined both by the economic and the broad non-economic social contexts which continuously change, and it, therefore, cannot be a static concept. Some of the recent studies by socio-economic anthropologists suggest that the grounds of this old food 'surplus' theory are much too generalized. "The concept of a superfluous surplus forces us into the fatal bias of believing that the rise of complex, stratified, and specialized socio-political organizations is dependent upon the production of food quanta which are 'unnecessary' and 'excessive' for the metabolic needs of the food producers. To confine evolutionary processes of such magnitude and fundamental morphological significance to the appearance of superabundant food supplies

is to fly in the face of the most central of all evolutionary doc-
trines: the superiority of reproductive potential over productive
ability. . . The belief that specialization and stratification arise
when the labour force produces more food than it needs to survive cannot be reconciled with the fact that, largely as a result
of malnutrition, the majority of the world's food producers have
never survived beyond infancy or early adulthood . . . (it arises)
from a failure to meet the additional requirements imposed by
the socio-cultural order. . . According to the dictionary, surplus
is 'that which remains when use or need is satisfied; excess'.
In using this term anthropologists have consistently committed
two errors: we have failed to make explicit the need which was
satisfied and we have failed to define the time period during
which the state of satisfaction persisted. As a result we have
been blinded to the fact that food quanta judged superfluous
from one viewpoint may be absolutely vital from another viewpoint and that excess quantities for short periods may be accompanied by drastic shortage over a long period".[76] This we
know is true in the case of India where throughout its history
and even today, there has been no 'progress' in any evolutionary
sense despite all the 'leisure' time peasants are supposed to have
by giving the so-called 'surplus' food to the non-agricultural
elite. Throughout the long history of famines in India it is
always the agricultural population that suffers the most because
it has to part with 'surplus' food.

"From what has just been said, it should be clear that there
is no reason to expect a one-to-one correlation between a particular level of surplus above subsistence and a particular degree
of specialization and social stratification. Others of a techno-
environmental nature may intervene. These in turn may be
responsible for the presence or absence of prior organizational
features essential for the predicted correlation between the
nature and size of the surplus and the phenomena of stratification and specialization. . . The notion of superfluous surplus. . .

raises the difficult question of why the group of food-producers should bother to produce superfluous food rather than merely cut back on their productive effort... Or why is the supposed increase in 'leisure' time devoted to specialized activities rather than to generalized indolence?... There is not the slightest evidence to show that the food-producer is any better fed in non-industrial stratified societies than among unspecialized, egalitarian groups. Stratification is thoroughly compatible with a static or even reduced level of food consumption per food-producer... When surplus is understood to mean necessary rather than superfluous food supplies, the question of incentives for the expenditure of superfluous effort no longer need occupy the center of attention. The reason food-producers keep on working is that despite (or perhaps in some case because of) the presence of a nonfood-producing class and abundant leisure, there is a shortage of necessary food supplies. The decisive question now becomes: what force or incentive makes the food-producers surrender a portion of their necessary food supply in order to support a class of nonfood-producers?

"Undoubtedly, the diversion of food from the food-producing group has not been accomplished in any single uniform manner throughout the world. But wherever we find a nonfood-producing elite, we may assume that they exist by virtue of their ability to control food supplies. Whatever the initial context of this control, once established, it is probably increased in direct proportion to the size of the surplus above subsistence produced by the food-producers and to the increase in the total population. This is because in the pre-industrial world, control over food amounts to the only effective source of culture-energy, energy in the literal thermodynamic sense—without which neither stones nor men can be moved".[77]

Thus, in the light of the above statement it becomes incumbent upon archaeologists to understand the socio-cultural organization of the Harappan society before anything specific may be said with regard to the subsistence-economic base in terms of the surplus theory. Furthermore, along with the problem of surplus food which is essential for the full development of a civilization in its concept of the urban definition, there is also the associated problem of understanding the general increase in agricultural efficiency that is imperative for the proliferation of the non-agriculturists. But, again, there has been little attempt by archaeologists to find ways and means to obtain a knowledge of the possibility of the intensive land use by the Harappans. For instance, intensive agriculture is generally associated with canal irrigation. But the possibility that canal irrigation was practised by the Harappans seems very remote both because it is, to be sure, extremely complex and in view of the evidence that is known today. Intensive large-scale canal irrigation requires the use of the plough that is not in evidence so far, and there is only the evidence of the harrow which can be "recognized as a common Indus ideograph symbol while there is no plough symbol".[78] Intensive agricultural methods also imply technical and social demands of a complex social order, such as the mobilization of masses of labour from many different communities whose activities need close cooperation. This close cooperation, in turn, involves the problem of maintenance and the demands of central supervision, in the form of a super-ordinate 'authority' which will see to the equitable distribution of water. Moreover, this form of social order has a tendency to constantly expand its urban area. But in the Indus Valley sites the limits of the urban areas appear to stay constant throughout, and as yet there is also no evidence of a super-ordinate 'authority' such as is clearly the case in Mesopotamia where the ultimate authority rests with an administrative elite. The "centralization of Sumerians, initially perhaps the result of agricultural need, was intensified because of military and industrial demand... What a contrast meets our eye when we view the Harappan civilization in the light of Sumer... Most striking is the fact that in contrast to a multiplicity of urban sites we have a majority of village sites... If one draws a 30 mile circle with Mohenjodaro at its centre, one finds villages such as Lohumjo-daro, Kot-Diji, and Jhukar encompassed. Further, in wandering north or south from the 'citadel' of Mohenjodaro, one encounters any number of detached sites in each direction... *Thus Mohenjodaro lies at the heart of a cluster of smaller settlements and this cluster appears to become denser as one moves to the centre"*[79] (Italics mine).

Therefore, what seems most probable, in view of the settlement pattern of Harappan society's urban areas, is that canal irrigation and intensive cultivation were absent and there were present more than one form of small-scale irrigation methods which seem to have sustained the subsistence-economic base of Harappan society. This seems to have been the case throughout the history of the urban sites of Harappan society, at least in the Indus Valley, where the use of different small-scale irrigation methods appears more plausible not only in view of the known archaeological evidence but also in terms of what one knows about the functional relationship between subsistence economic base and socio-cultural growth. The small-scale irrigation methods which were most probably employed are as follows:

(1) Wells, which are archaeologically attested by their presence in many of the houses at the Harappan urban sites.[80]

(2) There, most probably, was the construction of short-length canals in order to increase the flooded areas that would have served small landholdings. This is suggested by the archaeological evidence of the construction of dams at such sites as Amri and in the Las Bela region.[81] These small dams are very likely to have been prone to destruction by silting and flooding. But such small dams can be quickly and easily replaced because it does not represent any heavy involvement of labour.

(3) It is well known that the annual flooding of a river, specially the Indus and its tributaries, raises its beds and banks. It is also known that small-scale cultivation on this rich flooded soil has been carried on ever since man began to 'produce food'. In fact, in India, this method of cultivation is carried on even today, and a good crop from it is able to sustain a small town or a large village. Therefore, this also was probably an important and a chief method of irrigation for the Harappans.

Let us now attempt to infer the possible socio-cultural implications from these small-scale irrigation methods. The first inference is that these methods do not require a very elaborate social organization such as was required for large-scale canal irrigation in West Asia. The labour resources required for these irrigation methods need not have been larger than those that were already at the disposal of the individual community, kin group or even a family. Second, these operations may have been carried out through a pattern of reciprocity and small-scale irrigation methods probably only encouraged social stratification that was based on small landholdings.[82] Third, the presence of small-scale irrigation methods in the Harappan economy also implies that the subsistence-economic base was not dependent upon a single crop surplus of wheat, but most likely also on a diversity of resources such as other grains, dates, fish, fowl, animals, vegetables, fruit, etc., which are all evidenced by archaeology. This broad-based subsistence base must not only have ensured protection against natural calamities, but it must also have been essential for the long-term cultural growth and sustenance of Harappan society. Nevertheless, such subsistence on a diversity of food resources also requires redistributive institutions which, in turn, must have enhanced the growth of some form of a centralized 'authority' that we know is reflected in the archaeological evidence of granaries, citadel, etc. This central 'authority' in Harappan society must also have been necessary, at the same time, for the development of trade, exchange, etc., for which we have a great deal of evidence over a wide area.

The support for the presence of some sort of central 'authority' may also be inferred by the presence of the grid-pattern[83] of town planning which clearly implies a prior thought-out plan, and is not accidental. (This planning, as we learn from archaeological evidence, was carried out by means of precise instruments of measurement, etc.) The presence of a central 'authority' is essential in order to plan out a town with a predetermined scheme of streets, lanes, and in which the property is apportioned in rectangular plots, etc., so that any urban area may function as an organic whole. The grid-patterned town cannot be the result of a natural growth in response to the desires of individual builders, which is commonly noticed in the development of haphazard towns in later India and even today. Moreover, it is only possible to plan the grid-patterned town in either a total new urban unit or a newly added subdivision. But these and other inferences take us beyond the problems of the subsistence-economic base, into the problems that are related to the inferences of the socio-cultural organization. Therefore, let us now turn to these problems below.

B. Problems related to the integration and the organization of Harappan society, in terms of understanding the Indian Style

An attempt to understand the integration and the organization of Harappan society has appeared very complex and difficult in the past because archaeologists and historians have done this on the basis of certain old concepts. For instance, the Harappan evidence has generally been made to fit within certain evolutionary and historical schemes which divide human groups either into *societas* (kinship society) or into *civitas* (civil-state-society). This "dichotomy seems to have survived in the thought of some modern social scientists, including the anthropological evolutionists Childe and White".[84]   Hence, it is no surprise to note that archaeologists have visualized the evidence, not in terms of any socio-cultural interpretation of the persistence, spread and expansion of Harappan society, but as an 'empire' in which is present the characteristic political institution that one may expect to find in a 'civil' society.   But any such political institution could only have maintained itself by a readily available force in a 'civil' state.   However, in view of the subsistence-economic base noted above, Harappan society had very little chance to establish itself like the 'city-states' of its contemporaneous West Asian society.   Consequently, there has been a great deal of confusion in understanding the problem of a society such as the Harappan one which is, in fact, a 'transitional' one, in terms of the two categories of the old evolutionary scheme.

However, the old line of interpretation was also given because the Harappan evidence was often compared to the city-states and political empires of West Asia where it is probably correct to surmise that there had evolved a political class in whose hand authority was legitimately constituted.   Nevertheless, even in the case of West Asia, the problem was earlier viewed in terms of the political and social theories that are appropriate for a modern industrial society, that is, the concept of legal power or 'authority' which is a comparatively recent development in the history of human societies.   At any rate, it should be borne in mind that when one speaks of 'authority', it is erroneous to confuse it with the use of physical force because such a force can never sustain a given social system for a great length of time.   "Since authority always demands obedience, it is commonly mistaken for some form of power or violence.   Yet authority precludes the use of external means of coercion; where force is used authority itself has failed".[85]

Nevertheless, even if one eliminates the presence of a central 'authority' in the form of a 'governmental' or 'legal' institution, the problem still remains of defining and explaining what this form of central 'direction' or 'agency' was in the Harappan society, because we have already shown that it had existed. This means that we must examine the possible socio-cultural institutional means by which integration was achieved, and specially the motivating forces which must have enabled this non-coercing 'authority' to effectively act upon the individual members of this society. In this context, it will be appropriate to first note the functional prerequisites of human societies, that is, what are broadly the things that must get done in any given society (such as the Harappan) in order for it to be a going concern. Anthropological literature mentions an exhaustive list of these prerequisites. But, in the main, there are five broad categories of the underlying ends which tend to serve the broadest range of human activities, and are common to all human social groups. These categories are as follows:[86]

(1) To maintain the biological functioning of the group members.
(2) To reproduce new members for the groups.
(3) To socialize new members into functioning adults.
(4) To produce and distribute goods and services necessary to life.
(5) To define the 'meaning of life' and maintain the motivation to survive and engage in the activities necessary for survival.

This is a general scheme which should be borne in mind as a very broad frame of reference by archaeologists and historians whose ultimate concern is with 'real' human societies. It indicates to us that human societies function, or are governed, not so much by force or fear of physical restraint as "by what proper roles they should play in the status, position they occupy. In short, the vast body of social control is maintained through the internalization of social norms. Most of us rarely see the acceptance of social norms as a device for social control and order".[87]

In view of this the internalization of the socially accepted rules in Harappan society must have been very important, even though there may have been a body of physical restraints, if only in order to protect the arterial trade routes from raids and invasions. But in the absence of physical force and restraint or any sophisticated political institutions, there must have been certain crucial categories that maintained, motivated and perpetuated the rules and norms for hundreds of years in the apparently 'steady state' of Harappan society. Once again, if we turn to anthropology for help, we learn that in all human societies there is present the master category of ideology which generally acts as the motivating force and is intimately associated with the behaviour of individuals of any given society. Ideology has been defined as the conceptual organization of rules, taboos, laws, precepts, philosophy and values. In general, ideology has "its function of preserving the integration of the whole society. And it may be, too, that the longer a society is integrated in stable conditions, the more adjusted its parts become, and its people to each other, until no *overt* constraint (that is, coercion) is noticeable. . . Values are set down by tradition and are not usually questioned or even accepted consciously: a child grows up and becomes human among them. Thus values are inherently conservative. . . Ideology is preeminently cultural . . . for they (ideology rules) are directly symbolic in origin as inventions and as subsequent conventions".[88] It was thus, probably, ideology which was the chief motivating force in the internalization of the norms of Harappan society, and to this important problem we shall return later on.

We must first specify within a conceptual scheme, the particular forms of this society, which may be considered as 'transitional' within the dichotomy of *societas* and *civitas*. But for our purpose, the scheme that seems to appropriately fit the evidence is the evolutionary scheme of human social organization, as developed by Service. In this scheme there are five qualitatively distinct categories, broadly speaking, of the means of integration. In brief, these five levels are as follows:

"(1) Familistic levels of kinship and marriage which by their nature can integrate only relatively small and simple societies that we call bands;

(2) pan-tribal sodalities which can integrate several band-like societies into one;

(3) specialization, redistribution, and the related centralization of authority which can integrate still more complex societies;

(4) the state, further integrated by legal force; and

(5) an industrial society integrated not only by a state apparatus but also by a complex network of specialized, interdependent occupations".[89]

In this evolutionary scheme of social organization, the third stage seems to fit in most appropriately with the known archaeological evidence of Harappan society. The distinguishing features of this third level may now be stated.

This third stage which focuses attention on the rise of socio-politico innovation has been termed as the 'chiefdom' society and it has been defined as "largely familistic but is not egalitarian; it has no government but does have authority and centralized direction; there is no private property in resources or entrepreneurial market, commerce, yet there is unequal control over goods and production; there are rank differences but no clear socio-economic or political classes... Considerations of birth tend to dominate chiefdoms at every social level, from the status of individuals in a family to the relation of families to others, kin group to kin group, and so on... The basic ordering of this society should be hierarchical and composed of individuals, families, kin groups or villages, lineages which are unlike each other. The relations, expectations, forms of etiquette, frequently even the kinds of dress and ornamentation prescribed for each extend, make explicit and emphasise social differences. . . Sumptuary rules and the emphasis on rank are prominent".[90] These sumptuary rules include certain items of dress, ornamentation, perhaps kinds of food, that are reserved for one stratum and tabooed to the other.

In the above definition of a 'transitional' society, many of these characteristics may be seen in the known evidence of the Harappan society. For instance, it has already been established that it was a redistributional society, without the presence of any distinct 'political class' that might have exercised 'legal' force. However, it did have a central 'agency' for the coordination and distribution of products, and this is corroborated by the evidence of the 'citadel' area at the same location for hundreds of years. How was this possible ? This is where the importance of ideology comes in, because it made possible the perpetuation of the central 'agency', generation after generation, without the use of legal or other legitimate force. This central 'agency', once it had come into existence, in the absence of legal or physical force, could only have continued through sanctified, legitimatized and codified rights, privileges, etc. Hence, it must have also become imperative for this 'elite' class to prescribe the form of succession, within the ideological framework, which arrangement is particularly important in order to maintain the hereditary continuity of this 'post' from generation to generation. This hereditary 'post', once it came into existence, must have helped to foster and preserve the integration of Harappan society for the sake of integration alone.[91] However, the continuity of this 'post' alone could not have achieved social integration, because associated with the perpetuation of the central 'authority' is the fact that the entire structure of Harappan society must also basically remain the same; that is, it is equally important to maintain the stable continuity of generations of the remaining social classes, through the very same prominence given to the genealogical conception of succession as was the case with the 'elite' class. The archaeological evidence of the so-called 'monotonous' repetition in the same location of architectural features, other material traits and items, and the lack of the expansion of the urban areas, etc., very strongly suggests that this could have been only possible if prominence was given to the idea of 'succession', perpetuation of 'tradition' and the like. Thus, for all the sections or classes of this society the accurate calculation of genealogies for a great number of generations, specially in order to maintain the socio-economic and socio-cultural order, must have been a chief and important means to differentiate between people of 'high' rank (those who were interested in the retention of that 'office'), and those others of 'lowly' birth.

In short, Harappan society was most probably integrated and "stabilized by strict rules of hereditary succession and sanctioned by mythology, custom, values and so on, then to the extent that these are strong and consistent so is the authority strong and consistent".[92] The ruling 'elite' class was very probably maintained by descent reckoning, etc. (within the ideological framework), and in a similar manner the other social classes of specialized occupational groups must have been maintained through myth, ritual, sumptuary rules, etc. It should, however, be noted that this 'elite' class has, in fact, been envisaged by other writers as the 'priestly' class. But this could not have solely been a form of religious 'authority' because at this evolutionary stage of a 'transitional' society the twin powers of 'political' and 'religious' 'authority' do not function as separate institutions. Thus, the central 'agency' of Harappan society must have served many different functions, such as the social, political and economic ones, in addition to the religious one.

The basic characterizations of some of the features of Harappan society that have briefly been stated above appear to be very familiar in terms of some of the characteristic institutions by which Indian society (Style) is distinguished from any other society. These are as follows:

(1) There is the unique institution of caste by which a major part of Indian society has been, and still is, structured and organized. Therefore, let us pertinently digress a moment to briefly examine the current usage and definitions of caste. These are based on some 'recent' field studies by social scientists, instead of the commonly known old concepts and definitions of caste which are of not much help to us because in these definitions a great deal of emphasis was laid on some very erroneous notions. For instance, in 1908 Risley had "stated that the conquering Aryans behaved towards the conquered Dravidians in the same way as some planters in America behaved towards the African slave from where they were imported".[93] Similarly Keith, following Risley, was also of the opinion that in India 'races' were transformed into caste, that the processes of racial fusion were arrested long ago and, therefore, no national type could develop in India as in Europe ! [94] Many writers, archaeologists, historians and anthropologists have continued to follow this old definition and concept of caste. But, according to the now generally accepted definitions, as formulated by social scientists, the basic reason why caste is a unique feature of India is because of its emphasis on the religious aspects (and the ritual and myths associated with it), i.e., the 'ideological' aspect of caste. However, caste has also quite aptly been characterized as an hierarchy of endogamous divisions in which membership is hereditary and permanent. Therefore, caste-status is pre-determined because the system is perpetuated by birth and thus, membership in it is ascribed and unalterable. It is the absence of any radical or vital change in the caste system that is also of very important consequence because it makes a caste society, as a whole, an organic system within which each particular caste and subcaste fill a distinctive functioning role. Therefore, caste is also a

system of labour division from which the element of competition among the workers has largely been exhausted, and thus it is this fundamental fact of the economic interdependence that stems from the division of labour, which is also of quite a special type. Nevertheless, in all this, the role of religion is pivotal since it provides the ideological support to the caste system.

It is well known that the caste system constitutes, as has been stated above, one of the crucial social (institutional) features that give a distinct pattern to Indian culture and civilization. Therefore, it has been suggested, its roots must also be seen within these territories rather than in any worldwide cross-cultural generalization of caste and class.[95] But it should be borne in mind that caste society in India "is not a localized group, but comprises small local communities, often several miles apart. Local communities of different castes form administrative units as multi-caste villages or towns... India cannot be said to possess a single caste system, but a number of regional systems... Regional differences are related partly to ecological variation, and partly to political history".[96]

In any case, in the general context of seeking the roots of the institution, the above brief description of caste, as has been formulated from field studies, is very closely comparable to the inferences that we have already made with regard to the Harappan society. In short, we see a very early beginning of one of the most important social institutions of later India that characterize the Indian Style.

(2) Associated with the above characteristic institution is another essential component that continues so strongly in India today. This is the genealogical means of the perpetuation of caste status by birth. This characteristic, as we have noted, must also logically have been present in Harappan society.

(3) Another characteristic, which is also of considerable significance in Indian society, is the importance which is given to the memorization process, specially in descent reckoning, ritual

prayers, etc., which are all learnt by oral repetition. It is by the manner of memorization that 'learning' is passed on from generation to generation in India rather than by any elaborate written documents. It is well known that the continuity of the Indian Style has been maintained by remembrance and inheritance both in the realm of the 'secular' and the 'sacred' institutions. For instance, it was not until the second half of the 14th century A.D. that the Ṛg Vedic hymns were properly edited, written down and commented in South India. The text had till then been memorized syllable by syllable, but not generally committed to writing.[97] The oral means of imparting education is one of the chief means of learning even today, specially in the indigenous educational school system, and it is this process that has maintained and preserved India's traditional civilization. Once again, it is this characteristic of the Indian Style which may also be seen in Harappan society because we know about the unchanging script which had generally remained the same for many hundreds of years. But if, on the other hand, written documents were important, it would be normal to see at least some basic changes or evolution in the script. Moreover, even in the archaeological evidence there is, relatively, an acute paucity of written material, and there is no reason to believe why any *terra-cotta* written tablets etc. could not have survived just as the other *terra-cotta* objects have well survived. In the Indian context, therefore, it would be worth while for us to probe deeper into this problem of the absence of any elaborate written evidence.

The presence of writing has been considered to be one of the important criteria for the identification of the definitive stage of 'civilization' in an evolutionary scheme of classifying human societies. But, this old evolutionary device (which may hold good for the primary purpose of classification since in this manner one could designate the Indian or the Harappan society as a 'civilization') gives us very little idea of the status and role of writing which may have been given to it in a 'real' or 'functioning' society or social system. For instance, we all know that, today, in Indian society a knowledge of writing is present and its members are aware of the written word. But, by and large, in much of India's past, and even today, rituals, myths, 'literature', etc., have been orally perpetuated, through the memorization process. The knowledge of 'writing' in these 'caste-class'-structured societies is generally restricted to a certain extremely small privileged 'minority', and it does not play any essential role for the majority. The majority of Indians reside in villages and have been and are illiterate. They find little use for it. But as Redfield has said: "The peasant is also adjusted in ways that characterize his style of life, to that outstanding feature of civilization, writing. The precivilized hunter or villager is preliterate; the peasant is illiterate. The existence of the art of writing has become an element in the mode of life, although he himself perhaps cannot read or write. He must take account of those who can, and things written are meaningful objects in his life".[98]

Therefore, we may conclude that it is only for classificatory purposes, because the emergent forms are definitive, that writing is a goood criterion for classifying Harappan society as a 'civilization'. But in terms of its role in the socio-cultural integration and organization, written documents must have been of little importance either in the Harappan or even the later Indian society. It is the memorization process which is of great importance. This line of interpretation also enables us to explain why the form and pattern of the Harappan script had continued more or less to be the same throughout its history, with hardly any evolution or change. In case written documents had played an important role, as in West Asia, Harappan script should show us the normal evolution and change of its characters. It is, therefore, more likely that the seals were restricted to trade or to some other symbolic aspect of Harappan society, and writing was not part of the 'educational' or 'administrative' institutions. If there had been the extensive use of writing, then, other forms of seals, tablets, etc. should also have been preserved, along with the other well-preserved evidence that archaeology has managed to recover so much.

C. *Problems related to the spread of the idea of the peasant-urban Harappan system, and the possible process of origin*

The Origins: A brief reference to the problem of the transformation of communities living at the level of self-sufficient food-producing system into the level of the peasant-urban system is essential, before the problems related to the spread of the systems and ideas about the structure and organization of the Harappan system is considered. Until very recently, the majority opinion about the origins of Harappan society and civilization was that it must have been the result of colonization by West Asians: this is apart from the spread of the common pool of ideas (which were 'in the air') that probably did give rise to 'urbanization' in the fertile plains of the Indus. There are also various traits and items which are found at the Harappan sites that are often put forth to support the idea of an essentially West Asian nature of Harappan society. But these items and traits are comparatively few and rather suggest culture-contacts between the two areas, than any 'proper' colonization by the West Asians. The similarities in many of the items of the two areas are few, such as we see in certain art motifs as doves, snakes, and the ornamental forms of the repetition pattern, swastikas, kidney-shapes, etc., that are present on Harappan pottery. "Against this background the divergent pottery tradition in either region presents an archaeological paradox... The tools and armoury of the Indus Valley civilization also show absence of Sumerian influence. Filigree work, so popular in Sumer, was not much in evidence in the Indus

cities ... (the) ... as yet undeciphered Indus script has no
likeness to offer with the cuneiform or other scripts of West
Asia".[99]   Similarly, the isolated evidence of the famous bearded
man of Mohenjodaro in the DK area has been often interpreted
to represent the presence of West Asian 'elites' in the Indus
Valley. But even if this evidence, despite its ambiguous context,
is taken for granted, Wheeler has considered it to belong to the
late Harappan phases.[100]   Therefore, all these evidences only
provide proof of West Asian contacts, and do not establish the
fact that the nature or character of Harappan society was mostly
West Asian rather than Indian.

As opposed to this meagre 'West Asian' evidence, there is
now both archaeological and other 'indirect' evidence that the
development of Harappan society "was not the result of an
'explosive' descent into the lower Indus Valley nor the result
of a long occupation of that valley by that civilization. The
evidence is accumulating to suggest that not only was the
Harappan *the latest phase* of a long development within the
Indus Valley but that with more than a little probability it was
the *shortest lived* of these phases ... many of the characteristically Harappan traits have their proto-types in the earlier
cultures and that a process which I have called 'Indianization'
was at work to produce the characteristic features of the
Harappan Civilization... Taken as such the elaboration of
what appears to have been traditionally village culture (pre-
Harappan) was indigenous development... It is possible that
elaboration of ceremonialism may be a symptom of increased
precariousness of life in general which idea goes well with the
evidence for failure of local sources during the Harappan phase...
In any case, our evidence in the lower Indus Valley explicitly
indicates a long indigenous agricultural and technological pre-
amble to the Harappan Civilization. This further emphasises
the validity of the idea that the natural resources of Sind were
falling through over-exploitation which in time made natural

calamities such as flooding more disastrous and caused the gradual abandonment of the region".[101]

In addition to various new 'direct' facts of the pre-Harappan archaeological evidences which have been accumulating in recent years, the less 'direct' inferences with regard to the indigenous nature of various settlements must also be taken into account. For instance, during that time the grid-pattern development of town-planning was one of the characteristic features of Harappan society. But it is very important to note that this form of planning was not present at that time in West Asia. The grid-patterned planning, along with the development of 'sophisticated' trade with West Asia, implies that the Harappan urban areas had also developed very high quality manufactured goods, which could only have been possible through specialized classes with a long background of training and organization that was localized in a given area. Thus, in view of such 'facts' as well as of the recent archaeological evidence of the continuity of the several pre-Harappan phase features and elements into the mature Harappan phases (viz. at Kalibangan, Kot-Diji, Amri, etc.) it is more plausible to postulate that the ancestors of the people inhabiting the urban areas must have had a long history of the development of the specific form of social organization and integration in this very area and region.

This process of indigenous origins may now be stated within the general conceptual framework of Robert Redfield's,[102] summarized as follows:

'Civilizations' start up from their folk bases into specialized developments in which some elements of the folk society are left behind while others are retained. But the urban areas of 'civilizations' are different from the folk and peasant societies because of this coming together of different sedentary groups: there is now division of labour and the autonomous self-sufficiency of different groups is no longer as it was at the peasant or folk level. Instead of an exchange economy at the earlier levels there is now a redistributional economy because of specialization in skills of pottery, basket-making, weaving, carpentry, etc. This also results in the specialization of a family line; the job becomes hereditary and work becomes increasingly skilled. This is suggested and reflected by the continued residential occupation in one given area (as, for instance, is seen at many sites, such as at Chanhudaro which is a bead-makers' 'colony'). Therefore, with the increase in the degree of sedentariness of the residential groups, the chances are that more goods are now moved rather than people. Thus, according to Redfield, in the beginning of this transformation, the world-views of the two—the urban and peasant—are still at the bottom the same, but the complex conception of the literate, along with the increasing different economic systems of urban areas, now reaches far beyond anything of which the rustic could conceive. "This is the period in which the reflection and systematization accomplished by the literate have added a new dimension to the ethical and intellectual life. The moral order has now a public phase connected with deliberate policy".[103]

In short, the beginnings of Harappan society and civilization—in terms of the process of urbanization—may thus be seen as the transformation of the indigenous folk and peasant societies into a 'primary civilization'. But this process of (Harappan) origins or this transformation as conceived by Redfield, it should be borne in mind, was not at an end because once an urban society is established somewhat similar processes are involved in the 'secondary' spread of the now well-established peasant-urban (Harappan) system.

The Spread: We have already stated the possible institutional means of the internal maintenance of an organized and integrated Harappan society, as well as its origin, in terms of a socio-cultural framework and transformation. It is once again within this framework that we shall look at the spread of the peasant-urban system. For instance, we must remember (as anthropologists) that there are present in any human society not only certain inherent human needs and aspirations but also the quest for food and other economic needs etc. which are essential for biological survival. Therefore, in the case of an urban society with a food-producing economy which has facilities for storage, exchange, trade, etc., this society can neither remain 'static' in its needs and aspirations nor can it have a 'static' population. It must either diminish and fail from the very start or it must increase and spread. The demands of an urban society because of the redistributional nature of its economy are ever on the increase since it ceases to possess anymore the economic and cultural stability of the earlier self-sufficient folk and tribal societies. Moreover, the need for spreading out does not necessarily have to be only population pressure, food supply, etc., it can also be because of other cultural factors such as coming into contact and conflict with 'lower' cultures. The need to move and spread may also be conceived in terms of the ideological or the super-organic aspects which play a prominent role in urban societies.

The problem of finding adequate means of integration and of organization is of great importance, and it must also have been a continuous one in such peasant-urban systems. This expansion, specially the one which is correlated with the growth of population, also implies 'budding off' of additional groups. In short, what all this means is that similar to the processes of origin described earlier, there occurs now the voluntary incorporation of the neighbouring tribal and folk groups to participate into a redistributional society. But this incorporation does not necessarily mean the urbanization of neighbouring societies or the loss of their identity because this participation also means that as neighbouring peoples remote from the urban areas acquire more and more products and inventions of the 'city' they are no longer separate isolated entities.[104] Nevertheless, in this process of the spread and expansion and of 'budding off', etc., there is also the secondary phase of the procreation of other, perhaps smaller, urban areas which may have become secondary distributional centres. The recent archaeological evidence of the 'spreading' new sites corroborates this view albeit the new settlements not surprisingly show their own regional variations of the Harappan traditions.

Thus, we note that the spread and expansion of the Harappan system to the culturally 'lower' neighbouring areas was neither 'colonization' nor was it 'political' expansion of any form. It would rather be more appropriate to visualize this expansion in terms of the permeations of the socio-economic and socio-cultural systems of Harappan society. The beginnings of these permeations into further India, as we have already stated, may be seen in the trade, exchange, etc. pattern that had already been in existence, in some form or the other, from early pre-historic times. The evidence of exchange, 'trade', etc. for such early times is quite well known to archaeologists from all over the world, even at the hunting-gathering stages. The knowledge of old routes, of habitats, etc., which are generally improved upon by acquiring knowledge through various forms of contacts with the pre-existing earlier societies, is a well-known phenomenon. (For instance, this is the case even today because we see that railway routes and roads in India have generally been built along the millennia old ancient highways which, in turn, have probably had a prehistoric base.) Thus, the 'trade'-routes, patterns, etc. of the earlier food-gathering hunting and self-sufficient food-producing societies are regularized and normalized by an urban redistributional society in which trade-economy is an important aspect. In due course, there may be seen the traditionalization or normalization of relations between the 'higher' and 'lower' cultural groups in the expanding peasant-urban system, most probably within the already well-established socio-cultural system of the Harappans.

The implications, in terms of social organization, of this spread, expansion and 'budding off' of the families are that there is a tendency now for the distance from the original centre to correspond to rank differences among the local groups, and for genealogical distances to be "calculated in terms of the pervasive mode of primogeniture".[105] (This is yet another instance of an institution that is retained in later Indian society, such as the tradition of descent reckoning and the calculation of genealogies from some sacred centres.) It also means that as the branching and rebranching of the family structure progresses, it acquires greater autonomy and independence the further it moves away from the parental stem. Nevertheless, the connection with the central 'authority' is retained because it continues to be represented as a subsidiary 'authority' in the hands of one who has a knowledge of all the rules, norms, rituals, etc., which the 'elite' in the main centre are privileged to know. This subsidiary 'authority' then forms the permanent residential 'elite' both in the secondary towns and also in the villages.[106] Thus, we learn that in this expanding sphere of the peasant-urban socio-economic structure, there is also to be seen the spread of the Harappan institutions and ideologies into not only the 'secondary' urban areas but perhaps also into the self-contained villages which are not necessarily converted into urban areas but have nevertheless become part of the redistributional urban economy. It is by some such forms of spread and expansion that there also spreads the 'style of life'.

Hence, even if later on some of the urban areas like Mohenjodaro or Harappa had 'disappeared', the Harappan socio-cultural tradition and complex (or the 'style of life') must have remained preserved in the villages and small towns, i.e., there was the preservation, for instance, of such institutions as the 'caste-class' structure, of genealogical descent-reckoning, etc., as well as of the institutionalized resident stranger who is the representative of the urban 'elite' but who now becomes a part of the village structure.[107] It is most probably because of these reasons that many of the features seen in Harappan society are preserved throughout later India, and characterize the Indian Style.

To conclude this section, the problem of interpreting the archaeological evidence for the Harappan society has been viewed in terms of a functioning 'real' society. The Harappan society has been looked at as an organization of systems and institutions of activities which were accepted by the people not by force but by certain moral sanctions—ideology—through the various cultural devices such as myths, symbols, etc. Therefore, could we conclude about this ideology that the world-view of the Harappans was perhaps of a patterned kind, i.e., in this society the religious rites and functions of the 'priest'-cum-'ruler' and the various craftsmen and the other social classes had a duty to perform so that there was a functional relationship which had divine sanction ? The Harappans may have viewed their society as a part of a vast and complicated machine beyond individual comprehension in which all parts were somehow dependent and interrelated. Some such view may have formed the underlying vital element that maintained the system. But, of course, we can never hope to prove these 'ideological' aspects.

In any case, it is within the framework of the total functioning of human societies that the various material items of the 'archaeological societies' have to be viewed. But although this approach and suggestions may seem to be of a very ordinary obvious commonsense one, yet "they need to be asserted, however, if we are to connect, in some degree, the views of human history..."[108] It is within this view that the above attempt also enables us to understand the later Indian society in terms of the socio-cultural inferences that have been made with regard to Harappan society which, in the view of the author, forms the basis of the Formative Period of Indian society and civilization. It is within a similar approach—framework—that the problem of the 'end' of the Harappan society, survivals and continuities, etc. will be viewed in the next section, in order to see the persistence of the Harappan (Indian) Style.

PROBLEMS RELATED TO THE 'END', SURVIVALS AND CONTINUITIES OF THE HARAPPAN –INDIAN– STYLE

The 'end' of the Harappans in Indus Valley

There are many hypotheses which have been postulated to explain the end of the Harappans in the region of the Indus Valley. But of these, the one that postulates the destruction of the Harappans by the Aryans is a fairly well-known one, even though at none of the Harappan sites which have thus far been discovered is it possible to see this aggressive contact (in archaeological terms) between the Harappans and any of the 'post-Harappans'. In fact, even the evidence of the skeletons that were found in the topmost levels of Mohenjodaro and were supposed to represent a massacre by foreigners, is now considered to be a misinterpretation of the stratigraphy.[109] Nevertheless, taking the *Rg Veda* as it stands, there is same confirmation of the negative action of the ruin of some cities by Indra and his followers.[110] We shall return to this problem later on.

Another well-known postulate with regard to the end of the Harappans in the Indus Valley is the one that attributes it to 'natural' causes, such as the gradual worsening of the environment, and the encroachment of the desert due to desiccation, etc. This hypothesis which has been favoured by both Wheeler[111] and Piggot[112] finds little support since its validity is doubtful on the grounds of palaeo-climatology. The general consensus now is that ever since the end of the Pleistocene period, the natural physiography and climate have been relatively stable.[113] However, in spite of this, one cannot exclude the possibility of the local decrease in rainfall because of the change in the ecological balance i.e., because of the changing flora and fauna as a result of human activity. But any effects of the changing pattern of human activity on the land are extremely difficult to trace for any area for historic and prehistoric times, specially in quantifiable terms. But it is possible to state that deforestation was probably a major cause of much erosion which increased both the silt load and flooding potential of the Indus river. This, in turn, must have affected the construction and maintenance of any form of irrigation systems and, thereby, effected the continuity of occupation in the lower alluvium by the Harappans. But deforestation alone may not have been the cause for the upset in the ecological balance specially because there are no empirical data, as yet, for the rate of erosion at that time for the alluvial plain on the whole. Therefore, the causes of erosion may also have been various techniques of intensive cultivation, depletion of soil nutrients by inadequate crop rotation, and the disturbance of the natural patterns of drainage by the slow rise of the river bed and banks as a result of silting. All this would have caused some form of movement of the Harappan population. But even this hypothesis requires empirical evidence for the intensity of land utilization and of settlements pressing against any clearly defined cultural-ecological limits.

However, it seems more plausible to surmise that all these processes must have been going on simultaneously, to some degree. Nevertheless, any kind of answers to such problems require the understanding of ancient agriculture, such as it has been recently carried out for West Asia.[114] These studies are, by and large, absent in India except for the recent one which suggests that the increasingly frequent severe floods had in fact accelerated the silt deposits at the mouth of the Indus which had choked off Mohenjodaro from the sea, causing a rise in the water table that may have been a prime factor in the destruction of Mohenjodaro.[115] But it is not at all certain whether this process could also have been the cause of the end of Harappa which is situated far far away from the mouth of the Indus. Moreover, the chances of the total 'eclipse' of all of the Harappans because of this 'flood-silt' postulate are remote. The possibility of the total 'eclipse' is less evident outside of the Indus Valley, even in archaeological terms such as at Rangpur and some other sites in Saurashtra,[116] as has already previously been noted (Fig. 5). Here, the phases and levels suggest that there was a period of transition or some sort of a process of 'indigenization' of the typical Harappan elements rather than total destruction; that is, there was probably a time of reorganization and readjustment rather than what archaeological jargon has a tendency to call the 'degenerate' or 'impoverished local cultures', etc.

Nevertheless, strictly in terms of the archaeological interpretation of stratigraphy, the Harappans seem to have disappeared 'lock-stock-and-barrel' leaving only some unconnected material items in the form of 'survivals'. But this stratigraphic 'break', even though it may be a valid and correct interpretation of archaeological stratigraphy, leaves a great deal to be explained in terms of what one knows about the functioning of 'real' societies. For instance, it is difficult to imagine that the vast spread-out Harappan society and civilization, or the various networks of systems and institutions that were present, both in the villages and towns, simply disappeared in some mysterious 'romantic' manner. Now, if this had been the case, it would be difficult to explain not only the obvious elements that have filtered into later Indian society but also to explain the continuity, from Harappan days to our own, of the same 'physical' population composition in the regions of the Panjab, Gujarat and Sind. At any rate, in the empirical terms of archaeology, it is only as yet the transitional phases of the Harappan sites outside the Indus region which suggest that a process of probable social and culture-change was going on. But the evidence at the Indus Valley sites also suggests that the organization and the integration of the socio-economic and socio-cultural pattern of the Harappan systems were probably getting out of hand (socio-cultural change) with the spread of 'civilization' to the south and east of the Indus Valley. The Indus Valley sites clearly support this view of the internal break-up of the organization of control in such evidence as the lack of planning, untidy houses, use of old bricks, etc.[117]

In short, the suggestion here is that all these 'facts' of archaeology should be viewed in socio-cultural terms of culture-contact situations, acculturation, socio-cultural change, etc., i.e., in the light of some current socio-anthropological generalizations rather than in terms of extinction and replacement by a totally new system, or by different 'racial waves', etc. This manner of viewing the 'end' of Harappan society within our framework is important to bear in mind because it is within it that we should also attempt to understand the various traits of the Harappans and the other non-Aryan elements which have obviously survived into the make-up of later Indian society. Therefore, let us now deal with the problem of these survivals and continuities but only within the above framework, and not in the traditional manner of looking at these various traits as unconnected and unrelated elements that have survived due to historical accident, to merely form a trickle into the mainstream of the Indian Style.

Problems Related to 'Survivals' and Continuities

In archaeology, there is an accepted classificatory device of designating and identifying new 'cultures', in terms of an evolutionary sequential scheme, by the appearance of certain significant new traits which form the diagnostic elements for purposes of identification of the next 'new' stage, even though a majority of the older elements may continue within this 'new' stage or phase. But a fundamental error in methodology is committed when this classificatory device is also utilized for interpreting socio-cultural change. In this misinterpretation of understanding certain processual phenomena, the older traits in the new 'phase' or 'level' are given less importance and are considered as mere 'survivals', 'hang-overs' or 'dead weights'. The older 'material' or 'non-material' elements are generally interpreted as some form of fossilized items, that is, the older items are not considered any longer to have either a 'functional' socio-cultural base or to have acquired any new meaning in the changed socio-cultural context. However, such generalizations are grossly erroneous because one knows that just as socio-cultural systems and institutions require a certain 'material' base and 'environment' for their proper functioning, so do any material items and traits require a certain socio-cultural base for their perpetuation because, otherwise, neither any institutions or systems nor any material items would have shown long continuities in India. It is in this light, therefore, that the following evidence for the various 'survivals' and continuities should be viewed, and this has been divided into two parts, (I) archaeological and (II) textual.

(I) The Evidence from Archaeology

(A) In the previous section mention has already been made of the presence in the Harappan society of the intangible institutional aspects such as genealogical descent reckoning, some form of 'caste' structure and the importance given to memorization process, etc., which have survived into the matrix of Indian society. But we shall now mention the traits and elements of Harappan society, which may be called the 'direct' or 'tangible' evidences of archaeology, that have continued into later India. The 'tangible' evidences given below will also lend support to our earlier contention of the continuities of some of the basic Harappan socio-cultural features:

(i) There is continuity from Harappan times of the potter's wheel, carts and boats until today in Sind.[118]

(ii) The use of water jars, which are placed today in the water stalls in India, as well as the habit of throwing away the goblets of *terracotta* after use may be traced back to Harappan times.[119]

(iii) In Harappan architectural features there is to be seen the use of stucco which continues into later India;[120] and at Kalibangan, for instance, identical methods of house-building techniques are used today in the same region as was the case during Harappan times.[121]

(iv) The practice of building ritual bathing tanks and of the large number of bathrooms (but no lavatories) which is seen in the Harappan evidence, seems to have continued into India today.[122] There are other ritual items and cults of Harappan society such as the mother-goddess, *lingas*, yonis, 'proto-Śiva', swastikas, which have become a part of later 'Hinduism'.[123]

(v) The Harappans probably had a flourishing trade in ivory, precious items and cotton that were exported to West Asia. These items of export seem to be of similar importance even in historical times.

(vi) The beginnings of binary and decimal system and other measurements and weights which were used by the Harappans have continued into later India.[124]

(vii) There are some other items which have continued to be of use even today, such as dice, *kohl* (*kajal*) for the eyes that was kept in jars with sticks in them, ivory combs, bangles, and the use of garments for both men and women that needed no pinning.

(viii) There is a close relationship between certain modern breeds of Indian cattle and those depicted 4000 years ago on the seals of Harappa and Mohenjodaro. This evidence also hints at the social, cultural and environmental continuum of life in India. "One of the most widespread features of cattle-worship is the way in which beasts are adorned or decorated. . . Such painting is still to be found almost throughout the subcontinent, particularly upon festival days such as Holī,

Govardhan, etc. . . There is every suggestion that such painting of cattle is very ancient. Among the *terracotta* figurines of cattle of Chalcolithic age from Kulli painting is not uncommon. . . Other decorative features are strings of beads, of *terracotta*, even glazed, around the neck . . . such collars bear a striking resemblance to the collars depicted upon some Harappan seals . . . cattle sports are not only widespread in modern India, but they are sufficiently ancient . . . (they were) . . . in vogue in the cities of the Indus civilization . . . cattle fairs are also ancient . . . and are held at the time of some festival, usually one associated with cattle, at a spot which has some religious associations, and usually having a number of shrines and temples. . ."[125]

(B) There is also some *meagre* 'direct' archaeological evidence of the continuity of the characteristic Harappan traits and elements. The continuity of these in the non-Harappan trait-lists is seen in the various post-Harappan 'cultures' despite the obvious evidence of the archaeological 'break' which implies a disappearance of the Harappans. We have already noted the transitional levels in the Kathiawad 'cultures', and such is also the case at Jhukar,[126] etc. But this evidence—meagre though it may be—not only suggests a shift of the Harappan focus to the south and east of the Indus basin, but it also suggests an evident process of socio-cultural change. This shift and change seem to have been taking place at a time when there were also present other 'chalcolithic' peasant communities near or at these new settlement areas of the Harappans. For instance, phase Ia at Ahar has been dated to 1725 ± 140 B.C. by C_{14}[127] and, similarly, the C_{14} dates from the lowest levels of the Black and Red ware phase at Atranjikhera probably suggest contemporaneity with the Late Harappan phases.[128]

The following are some of the other examples of the Harappan traits, and other borrowings that suggest the 'indigenization' of the non-Harappan 'cultures'.

(i) At Lothal, the 'Micaceous Red Ware folk' seem to have been living there for a considerable length of time, perhaps even before the Harappans had arrived. The evidence for this ware begins in the lowest levels, along with the Black and Red painted ware as well as the characteristic Harappan wares. The latter groups seem to have borrowed many of the local elements in their ceramic tradition. This borrowing suggests socio-cultural change (a 'regionalization' process) which is also suggested by the presence in the Harappan levels of new 'fire' and 'animal-sacrifice' cults, and by the presence of previously unknown joint burials.[129] (It may be noted here that there is also a suggestion of 'regionalization' or 'indigenization' of other non-Harappan 'foreigners' who came to India soon after the 'end' of the Harappans in the Indus Valley. This is hinted at by the evidence from the Jhukar settlements at Chanhudaro where the stamp seals, copper shaft-hole axe, etc. are definitely of alien tradition, but most of the ceramic tradition here is of an indigenous variety mingled with isolated motifs from further West. This is also the case at Cemetery H which belongs to a foreign tradition, yet it has a pottery tradition that is essentially indigenous albiet with West Asian motifs mixed in it.)[130]

(iia) The characteristic dish-on-stand, including the type with a corrugated stem, which fits in with the typical Harappan assemblage is to be found at a very much later date in the 'Red ware' assemblage at Ahichchhatrā. The corrugated type has also been found at Hastinapur in the Painted-Grey-Ware (PGW) levels,[131] as well as in the 'chalcolithic' assemblages at Nāgda, both these sites being of a much later date.[132] It should be mentioned here that the Painted-Grey-Ware has quite often been identified, on justifiable grounds, with a group of the 'Aryans', but there is no unambiguous identification or correlation for it as yet.[133] But whosoever these Painted-Grey-Ware people may be, they came into India at a time when it was already quite well populated. Therefore, it was 'natural' for them to take to the indigenous ways, such as we have seen of their adoption of the local ceramic styles, even though suited to their own 'taste'. But this adoption also significantly implies a taking-over of the indigenous institutions that are associated with a sedentary way of life. This problem will be discussed in the section below (II).

(iib) This 'indigenization' of the PGW elements is seen again at Ambkheri where a dull-red-ware has been found, "bearing relief decoration – wavy or ripple – which is met with in the late PGW as an associated type. It is this ware which continues in the subsequent period and thereby provides an important clue for the make up of the PGW culture."[134] This may be interpreted to mean that the PGW was an outside imposition, whereas the dull-red-ware was the indigenous element.

(iic) The evidence at Atranjikhera suggests this 'indigenization' even more strongly. Thus, in the PGW level, the Painted-Grey-Ware is the characteristic sophisticated pottery. But it forms only 3-10 per cent of the total complex, whereas the older elements of the plain Grey ware, Black and-Red ware and the dull-red ware (which was prominent as a wheel-made ware in the last phase) form the bulk of this main complex of the PGW level.[135] A period of socio-cultural change is, therefore, clearly indicated from the evidence of this archaeological level of 'transition', and this change may have been either of an 'internal' kind, or of an 'externally' stimulated socio-cultural change. This is further suggested by the fact that the PGW percentage is seen to gradually increase in the later sub-phases and, therefore, suggests its dominance, or what may be looked at as the strong emergence of the 'new' intrusive elements. Hence, this evidence in socio-cultural terms may also be interpreted as either the emergence of a new 'powerful' group from within or without, or of an 'elite' from within, i.e., there was now a social group of 'high' status which had reduced the other groups to a 'lower' status.

However, these are only hints with regard to the lines of approach because at this stage our aim is only to suggest that these problems should be viewed *not* in terms of displacement and disappearance of the old evolutionary or typological concepts; but that these problems be seen from the viewpoint of reorganization, restructuring, socio-cultural change, etc., as normally is the case with human societies.

(II) The Textual Evidence

The importance of the timeless features of India's villages has often been cited in the literature that deals with its civilization. Similarly, it is important to note the continuity of the various levels of society—of the survival of the various social layers of the many previous stages—and of the survival at the same time of the various cultural elements, traits, words, rituals, etc., in India. But there has been very little attempt to explain these features in terms of the retention and continuity of the basic socio-economic and socio-cultural institutional patterns. The explanations, if any, have generally been in terms of some 'higher' 'spiritual' ones, which has suggested to many that India at the 'lower' socio-economic levels is a 'hodge-podge' of a civilization. However, as we have stated earlier, there is a regular pattern of this stability and continuity not only because of the interrelatedness of the folk-village-town systems but also because of the presence of some important institutions, such as caste. The latter has helped to maintain the horizontal unity by cutting across its own regional vertical unity, through certain institutional ways of contact such as by means of the familial, sacred, commercial, fair or festivals, etc., as well as in terms of the various pilgrimage centres, myths, folklores, etc.

However, this fact of preservation and retention does not imply that there has been an ossification of the various levels of Indian society, because socio-cultural change is inherent in human societies. But depending upon the degree of change, social and cultural anthropologists have classified change in terms of some form of rearrangement or reorganization, or restructuring. In India's case, it seems that until now only organizational changes have been taking place and not the structural one, because if the latter had taken place there would have been a drastic break discernible in the long continuum of the Indian Style. Thus, for instance, an important organizational change that finally enabled the Indian Style to crystallize took place during the latter half of the Formative Period, with the coming of the 'Aryans' into India around the generally accepted date of 1500 B.C. Our opinion about this reorganization is contrary to the general consensus which is, that it was the 'Aryans' who Indianized the 'left-overs' of Harappan society and the sparsely populated 'primitive' aborigines who were present in India prior to their coming here. But, in fact, in view of what has been stated elsewhere in this chapter, there arose culture-contact situations with the coming of the 'Aryans', and it was the Harappan socio-cultural and socio-economic institutions which played a very fundamental role in the formation of what was later to be characterized as the Indian Style. The basic structure of the Indian Style had already been formulated, and it was over this that the tribes of the 'Aryans', with the probable superior language and technology of weaponry, had imposed or preferably 'acculturated' themselves. The chief reason for the view is that this 'contact', readjustment and change during the final phases of the Formative Period must be looked at in the light of the laws of social and cultural change as are currently valid. But before going into these implications which will be dealt with in the concluding part of this chapter, the following are some of the brief inferences and interpretations (which support the archaeological ones already stated) of the evidences from literary texts which suggest this process, i.e., the adoption by the Aryans of

many of the earlier Harappan (pre-Aryan) and other non-Aryan
socio-economic and socio-cultural institutions.

(A) "In spite of their practice of ploughing the Aryans are
known to have had only one variety of grain known as *yava*,
which may be taken as a generic name for the various kinds of
grain or in its later meaning barley. Cattle-raising most probably was a more important occupation, especially in the begin-
ing of the Vedic period ... but later the indigenous economy
and crops, diet, etc. were adopted".[136] Thus, by the time of
the Satapatha-Brahmana, in addition to barley, the chief
crop that was now produced was wheat, which we know was
already part of the Harappan economy just as it continues to
be the staple diet of the people of North India even today.[137]
Again, "it is for the first time during this period that rice, known
as *vrāhi*, appears in the Vedic texts".[138] Rice, however, is not
an 'Aryan' grain and it implies the gradual but very important
change that was being brought about by the indigenous elements, such as wheat and rice, into the Aryan economy, and
thereby in the socio-cultural organization.

(B) Cotton, which we know was present at the Harappan
sites and was most probably part of their trade, was not known
to the Ṛig Vedic Aryans, but wool is mentioned.[139] We also
know that it is cotton and its products that gain considerable
importance in later Indian economy.

(C) Similarly, the "Ṛig Vedic word for potter, *kulāla* has no
parallels in other Indo-European languages, which might suggest
that the Aryans adopted the local traditions in pottery".[140]
In fact, pottery gains so much importance later on (we have
already stated the archaeological evidence for this) that by the
time of the *Satapatha-Brahmana* pottery is almost used like a
currency, and even an offering of eleven potsherds is given as a
sacrifice to Agni over a land dispute.[141]

(D) The changes in the subsistence-economy, social order, etc.,
of the known Aryan society, such as have been indicated above,

were also taking place in trade and commerce which, probably, was also adopted from the sedentary economy of the pre-Aryans. Trade and commerce are not part and parcel of any migratory pastoralists, and this was the case with the cattle-raising economy of the earliest Aryans. The support for the 'non-Aryan' nature of trade and commerce is also seen in the Vedic texts in which one of the non-Aryan peoples mentioned are the *Panis*. This name does not "seem to be Aryan, but the word left important derivatives in Sanskrit and through Sanskrit in later Indian languages. Trader, modern *bāṇiā* comes from the Sanskrit *vaṇik,* which in turn has no known origin except in Pani . . . Coin is *paṇa* in Sanskrit; trade goods and commodities in general are *panya.*"[142] But the very incorporation of this non-Aryan term and its derivatives is of great significance since it clearly implies the adoption of 'foreign' social institutions, ideas and concepts. It is only within the social context that the name or word could have continued to increasingly function, and we already know that trade and commerce were important aspects of Harappan society.

(E) The earliest evidences for weight-standards for Indian coins are exactly those of a definite class of weights that were found at Mohenjodaro, and these are not the standards prevalent in Persia and Mesopotamia. "Regular coinage had come into use before the end of the seventh century. . . The eastern standard weight for silver coins was the *kārshāpaṇa* of 3·5 gms weight in Magadha, while the solitary Kosalan hoard known was of 3/4th *kārshāpaṇa* standard. The weight goes back to the Indus Valley culture which had, in fact, produced accurately cut stone weights of just this magnitude".[143] Similarly, the punch-mark characters on silver blanks are derivable from the Harappans, whose descendants were the Panis, according to Kosambi.[144]

(F) In the early Vedic literature, with reference to settlement patterns, there is no evidence of the varied "socio-economic

groups living in one village, since each single village was presumably inhabited by a group of families belonging to the
same class and following the same occupation which was mainly
agricultural and pastoral in character. . ."[145] On the other
hand, we know that settlement patterns which are based on
occupational social differentiation were present in Harappan
society. Therefore, it is "permissible to conjecture that the
Vedic Aryans had adopted or were obliged to adopt this pattern
of occupational village".[146] This form of settlement pattern
of many villages and small towns continues even today, that
is, it is in accordance with this idea of the concentration in
specific localities of the various occupational social classes,
much like was the case at Harappa and Mohenjodaro.

We have already stated, earlier, that the idea of this plan
of settlement patterns had also spread into the villages and
towns through the peasant-urban Harappan system. Therefore, even if the 'big' cities of the Indus did disappear, the
Aryans must have come into contact with the peasant-urban
system in the other small towns and villages where these patterns were probably retained. Anyway, this reorganization and
acculturation etc. of the Aryans in terms of the adoption of
the indigenous settlement patterns and, therefore, the social
systems probably resulted in the crystallization of the socio-
economic aspect of the Indian Style. The incorporation into
the Aryan sacred texts of this social differentiation had by
500 B.C. formed into the system of *jati*, or what is later called
caste.[147]

(G) In the method and technique of house construction,
the regional survivals until today of the traditional pre-Aryan
forms at such sites as Kalibangan etc. are fairly well known.
But this regional continuity from pre-Aryan times cannot simply
be explained only on technological grounds of the availability
of raw materials, such as bamboo, reeds, straw, wood, stone,
etc., which are accessible locally. If this continuity has been

possible it is because of the continuance as well of the socio-
economic structure of the villages which is reflected in the occupational settlement patterns and house types.

Therefore, it is within this context of the social system that
the adoption by the nomadic-pastoralist Aryans of the Harappan economy, settlement patterns, etc., should be viewed. In
fact, the *Ṛg Veda* says nothing about fixed settlements, art,
architecture, etc.[148] Moreover, it is generally accepted that
the *Ṛg Veda* was written in India, after the Aryans had been
in the north-western part of the subcontinent probably long
enough to have taken to sedentary agriculture habits and settlement patterns. Thus, it is not surprising to note that it
is only towards the end of the Ṛg Vedic period there is evidence
that agrarian economy had become more stable.[149] This the
'Aryans' must inevitably have acculturated from the already
settled pre-Aryan communities albeit remoulded or remodelled
according to their 'ideology'.

(H.i.) It is known that the Aryans were not city-builders, and
the early literary texts of the Aryans also suggest that city-
building was not a social activity in which the Aryans were
proficient.[150] In the *Ṛg Veda*, as is known from the writings
of many authors, the destruction of the ninety-nine *puras* of the
Asuras seems, most probably, to refer to the *puras* of the
Harappans. Moreover, the "oldest Sanskrit word denoting city,
i.e., *pura*, is usually derived from the Dravidian *pur*. . . The
word nagara too is found but only as a derivative adjective . . .
for the first time in the sense of a town in *Taittiriya Āranyaka* . . .
certainly much more frequently in later Sanskrit literature.
From the use of the adjectival term *nagrim* in the Aitareya
Brāhmaṇa as well as in the *Jaiminya Upanishad*, it appears
that towns of some description had already come into being".[151]

(H.ii.) City-building, etc., as a large-scale socio-economic
activity, is only much later mentioned in the texts such as the
Epics, Purāṇas and the early Buddhist and Jain texts. "It is

also very significant that in later Sanskrit traditional literature of the *Itihāsa-purāṇa* class, i.e., in the Epics and Puranas, large-scale building activities are invariably associated with the *daityas*, *dānavas* and *asuras* who were presumably of the pre-Aryan and non-Aryan stock... One has only to refer in this connection, to such names as Maya-dānava and Viśvakarmā. It is further significant that in the Brahmanical caste system architects, builders, sculptors, etc., along with other craftsmen are always listed low down in the social scale. It has, therefore, been suggested that town-planning and city-building as organized and recognized social activities were adopted by the later Aryans from civilized pre-Aryans... This adoption may have followed the gradual transformation of the pastoral-agricultural economic order characterized by a mixed economy based on agriculture on the one hand and trade and commerce, also crafts and industries, on the other".[152]

(H.iii.) It is only in the second century B.C. in the Milinda-pañha that an elaborate description of a city is found in which the architect "searches out first a faultless pleasant spot ... to be laid out into rectangular measured quarters, with excavated moats and ramparts on all sides, with high towers and strong gate-houses, with cross-roads, street corners, market-places and public squares",[153] etc. (This reminds one of the planning of the Indus Valley cities.) Nevertheless, as yet, "the attitude of sacerdotal Brahmanical texts does not seem to have been much in favour of the growth of towns..."[154] to this pre-Aryan habit !

(H.iv.) We know that the planners of the Harappan urban areas had separated the citadel from the other 'low' class areas in the Indus Valley. This separation of the area is, later on, also seen in 'ancient' India when "it seems that the city was not coextensive, in all cases and epochs ... with the citadel itself ... which were the residences of the king, his ministers, army chief, etc. while ... outside in the city there were the residences of lesser personages of the army, of merchants, and shops and markets, etc. The common people seem to have lived outside the city gates, or say in the villages. . ."[155] This planning is also very reminiscent of the Harappan towns.

(H.v.) Associated with this continuity and adoption by the Aryans of town-planning, method of construction, settlement patterns, etc., most probably from the non-Aryans and pre-Aryans, there is also the evidence of the adoption of certain non-Aryan ritual practices and observances which are inter-related with such house-building activities as the laying of the house foundation and of the first entrance into the dwelling houses. "Gradually they became part and parcel of Brahmanical rituals as exemplified by the *Gṛihya-Sutras* and are practised even today not only in villages but in towns. . ."[156]

(H.vi.) It is interesting to note, in passing, that during the Early Ṛg Vedic times Indra is very angry with the *dāsa* or the city-builders whose practice was to dam the waters. But very much later, by the post-Mauryan times, the Brahmanical law-books prescribe very stringent punishments for those who cause any harm to water reservoirs ! Thus, "Manu ordains that one who destroys the embankment of a tank should be either drowned in water or put to death by beheading".[157]

In this context, the importance of ritual tanks, 'great-bath', etc., of the Harappan society has already been stated. There-fore, it is also worth while to note the indirect "evidence of the popularity of tanks in North-Western India and U.P. is furnished by the practice of offering ritual tanks, which have been discovered at Taxila, Hastinapura, Udaipura, Ahichchhatrā, Kauśāmbī, Bhita, etc. . . . It has been argued that these votive tanks suggest Parthian or Indo-Parthian analogues, but Marshall's contention that these tanks were essentially Indian in character cannot be brushed aside lightly. . ."[158]

(J.i.) It has been suggested by us, earlier, that in the Harappan society the 'priestly' class ('agency') was of great importance as the central 'authority'. On the other hand, there is little evidence in the *Ṛg Veda* of any special importance which is given to the 'priests' as a class or a group. However, once again, we find that, later on, the 'priests' as a class assume a form of institutionalized authority. It is, therefore, important to note yet another example of this adoption, from the pre-Aryans, of an institution that comes into prominence later, along with many other institutions that have briefly been alluded to above.

(J.ii.) Associated with this rise of the 'sacred' institution of the 'priestly' class is also the adoption of certain non-Aryan gods and deities. It "is a fair guess that some of the peculiar Vedic gods not known elsewhere had been adopted from the pre-Aryans. The best known episode of the kind is victory of king Sudās—over the Ten-kings' confederacy. Sudās, called descendant of Pijavana, is also stated to be son of Divodāsa. The termination *dāsa* is curious . . . originally *dāsa* or Dasyu applies to a hostile non-Aryan people. . . Only after repeated conquest does the word *dāsa* come to mean slave or helot. . . That so early a name of an Aryan king should end in *dāsa* means that there was some recombination between Aryans and non-Aryans soon after 1500 B.C. The tribe over which Sudās was chief is given as the *Bhāratas*, or perhaps a special branch of the *Bhāratas* called Tṛitsus. . . These *Bhāratas* were definitely Aryans. Obviously, racial purity meant nothing to the early Aryans; adoption of the autochthones was always possible and practised. . . The priest who sings of victory over the Ten Kings has the clan name Vaśishṭha, still one of the traditional 'seven' major brahmin exogamous groups. The original priest had been Viśwāmitra of the Kuśika ('owl') clan. The priestly function was not as yet specialized to any one caste in the *Ṛg Veda*, and in fact the only caste difference in the earliest Veda was of colour, between light skinned Aryans and their darker enemies. . . Though the various specialized priestly offices at a fire sacrifice are listed, there is no brahmin caste as such with a monopoly of priesthood. Vaśishṭha, however, was a new type of priest . . . came of the human representative of a pre-Aryan mother goddess and as such had no father. Going over to the patriarchal Aryans required some respectable father and at the same time a denial of the non-Aryan mother. . . The seven main brahmin clan progenitors may go back to hoary Sumerian or Indus antiquity as the 'seven sages'; their names do not tally in the various lists given by brahmin scriptures. Viśwā-mitra is an eighth, the only genuine Aryan of the lot. The adoption of such 'jar-born' seers into the high Aryan priesthood was a fundamental innovation. By such recombination of Aryan and autochthone, a new class of specialists developed which would eventually claim monopoly of all Aryan ritual—the brahmin caste. . . There is Ṛg Vedic evidence for the germina-tion of a new professional brahmin priesthood that could serve more than one master at need, Aryan or not. A sage *Vaśa Aśvya* thanks the Dāsa kings Balbūth and Taruksha. . . The Aryan seer of another hymn thanks none other than 'Bribu', chief of the Paṇis, for the patronage. . ."[159]

(K) We have already noted the importance of dice and other games in the Harappan society, and it is seen that this gains considerable importance in the later hymns of the *Ṛg Veda* in which the gambler is described with his incurable passion and complete disregard for home and family.[160]

(L) Finally, it is a fair guess to state that the Aryan pastoral-ists were organized into a social organization which may be described as a 'tribal' one, in which a chief characteristic was their gathering together in stockades where the 'chief' normally dwelt. One cannot but help admitting that this form of social organization was not adequate to cope with the socio-economic and socio-cultural organization of the urban ('civilized') seden-tary life. Therefore, if perchance this tribally organized society had retained its characteristic form, one could hardly have identified it with what one can identify today in the Indian Style.

Thus, the early Aryan society, in order to become 'civilized', had adopted a host of the indigenous social and cultural systems, institutions, etc. of the already 'Indianized' inhabitants. A part of this process of the assimilation and the adoption of the indigenous gods, etc. has been very appropriately and interestingly described by the late Prof. D. D. Kosambi.[161]

CONCLUSION: THE PROBLEM OF THE COMING IN CONTACT OF THE ARYANS WITH THE NON-ARYANS AND PRE-ARYANS

In considering the genesis of Indian civilization it is generally accepted by a majority of scholars that the formation of the Indian Style or 'Indianization' took place, by and large, with the advent of the Aryans, around the most accepted date of 1500 B.C. The chief reason for this is the conventional approach and methodology of interpreting both the pre-Aryan and Aryan evidence, specially the characteristic stratigraphic 'break' that ends the Harappan assemblages at most sites. But along with this interpretation of Harappan stratigraphy, there is also the fact that over-emphasis has been given to the religio-philosophical thought by which the Indian 'way of life' is often characterized. Some of these scholars have also fallen into the trap of literally believing the writings of the Vedic Aryans who had themselves 'so sedulously propagated' the total conquest of the indigenous 'wretched *dāsyas*', by telling tales about the glorious victories of god Indra. Therefore, the idea of a discontinuity between the pre-Aryans and the Aryans has commonly been favoured, and it is generally thought that the 'Aryans' began a civilization almost *de novo*.

Hence, in terms of the traditional interpretation, the Harappa civilization, with its obvious stamp of the great Indus-river-Valley in whose lap it flourished, is considered by these scholars to have simply vanished. It is for these various reasons that even though the activities of the spade had already in 1921 brought the Harappa civilization to light, there has remained a sharp distinction between it and what was unmistakably considered to be the historic period of Indian society and civilization. The earliest moorings for the conventional historian, even today, is the annexation of the Indus Valley by Darius of Persia in the sixth century B.C., and the earliest datum line for historians is the year 326 B.C. when Alexander the Great invaded the north-western frontiers of the subcontinent.

Nevertheless, one cannot ignore certain new archaeological facts as well as the social science method and approach of interpreting the 'survivals' and continuities of a large number of pre-Aryan cultural items, and the very well-known mention of non-Aryan and apparently pre-Aryan elements in Vedic religious writing and poetry. One has to bear in mind recent archaeological evidence that indicates a vastly greater area of the spread of the Harappan evidence than was once believed to have been the case. There is now, as has briefly been mentioned elsewhere in this chapter, evidence that the regional variations of some of the complex Harappan assemblages may have persisted well after the sites of Harappa and Mohenjodaro were 'terminated' in the Indus Valley. In addition, for a somewhat later time, in the non-Harappan areas there is evidence of well-settled peasant villages spread throughout most of Central and Western India and, for slightly later still, in North-Eastern and Eastern India. Thus, as the archaeological picture emerges now, there is an impressive evidence of the overlap and interlocking of sites, assured by C_{14} dates, and by the associated finds recovered over vast areas. Hence, by the middle of the second millennium B.C. the entire subcontinent up to its borders appears to have been inhabited by interrelated settlements and not isolated self-sufficient villages. Some of the later non-Harappan sites even show borrowings of the Harappan tradition.

There are, of course, many authors who claim that the Harappan civilization is Indian, but they do so following an appeal which is primarily emotional, so as to give India a great antiquity. But there are a few archaeologists and other specialists who have suggested that there may be seen in the Harappan evidence the long continuities and antiquity of some aspects of the Indian Style. Thus, for instance, Wheeler has aptly concluded: "Did all they represent perish with them ? . . . What of their less tangible qualities, their philosophy and their beliefs ? Here archaeology is of necessity an insensitive medium. But reason has been shown to suspect that the later Hinduism, in spite of its Āryan garb, did in fact retain not a little of the non-Āryan, Harappan mentality and relationships, perhaps to a far greater extent than can now be proved. . . Paradoxically it would appear that the Indus civilization transmitted to its successors a metaphysics that endured whilst it failed utterly to transmit the physical civilization . . . Our appreciation of its achievement must in the end depend upon a marshalling of values. . ."[162] Similarly, on the basis of the survival of a large number of unrelated cultural items, Childe had reached this conclusion: "The Indus civilization represents a very perfect adjustment of human life to a specific environment. . . And it has endured: it is already specifically Indian and forms the basis of modern Indian culture . . . (it) . . . can only have been created and spread over a vast area after a long period of incubation on the spot".[163] But more recently, Fairservis has hinted at the correct method and approach of dealing with this problem: "Harappan is definitely Indian in its important features. One of these features, it appears is the peculiar situation of a society possessing civilization but dwelling largely in villages with ceremonial centralization, and decentralization for other purposes. What effect does this situation have upon the evolution of the culture involved ? What happens to new ideas and techniques when they are introduced into this cultural ground ? ... I am more than ever convinced that to know more about the Harappan culture we must know more about Indian village life".[164]

There are some others who have expressed the view that there was a synthesis between the various non-Aryan and Aryan elements. But for many of the scholars this synthesis has been viewed at some 'spiritual' level, and it has not been elaborated and understood within any socio-anthropological framework, i.e., within the socio-economic and socio-cultural structure of the functioning of 'real' human societies. Therefore, it is within the latter framework that the Harappan and non-Harappan culture-contact situations and the other evidences stated earlier have been viewed, rather than within the traditional historical orientation. It is only within this approach that it becomes possible to develop the theme of what Wheeler refers to as the 'metaphysics' and the 'marshalling of values'. One is only then able to trace the various aspects of the Indian Style and its essential ingredients of the basic institutions etc. from the Harappan times. This basic structure of Indian society had already been well formulated before the Aryans came to an inhabited land, and it was upon these earlier foundations of the Indian Style that the superstructure of the Indo-Aryan-speaking invaders, their religio-philosophical 'ideology' was probably built. In fact, the institutional patterns of the Harappan society, *which is pre-Aryan but not non-Indian*, are preserved in some form or the other even today in the smaller towns and villages.

The basic premise throughout this chapter has been that both the metaphysical and the 'material' (things, objects) world etc. are interrelated and neither can exist without each other nor endure and be transmitted without the socio-cultural and socio-economic systems of a given human society. Perhaps, it is a truism to state this. But this line of processual interpretation must be borne in mind in order to view the problem of the Aryan and pre-Aryan culture-contact situations, i.e., these have to be viewed in terms of certain acculturation processes, or socio-cultural change, which have been generalized from examples of ethnography and the currently valid laws of the pertinent social sciences. Consequently, let us now look at this problem of the appearance of the Aryans and their coming in contact with the 'indigenous cultures' in India, within our broad anthropological framework.

Thus, if supposing the claims of the Aryan texts are taken as literally true, i.e., about their overwhelming superiority and their vanquishing the aborigines, it would imply that there was a wide disparity between the two cultures, and that is why such a total conquest was possible. In this situation, therefore, it would be correct to assume that there was probably an aggressive meeting of the two and the results of such a culture-contact situation would probably have fallen within one of the following three possibilities. One, the total destruction of the native culture; two, the transformation of the native culture; and three, the total incorporation of the native culture within the invading culture.[165] However, in the previous section it has been shown by means of archaeological and textual evidence that there was not any such great disparity, on the whole, between the two cultures as the Aryan texts may imply. If anything, it may be said that the Harappans were in a very much 'advanced' state of 'civilization'. Thus, these three alternatives of the culture-contact situations are not of much help in this case. These alternatives would probably hold good, for instance, in culture-contact situations that had developed between the European settlers who came in contact with the American Indians, and the result of which, we know, was the almost total destruction of native cultures.

The case of India, at this stage of the Formative Period, was quite different. It is well known that India has often been called the 'melting pot of cultures' and we have noted that all kinds of 'cultures' and 'societies' continue to exist side by side. But this is not a case of coexistence because whenever new 'cultures' have entered India, they have adopted the indigenous institutions and systems of society even though their super-structure of ideology has been retained. There are several instances of this process, and the commonly observed example that may be given is that of the 'tribals' of India who, whenever they are converted to any of the great religions, their 'ritual' frame of reference is retained. Again, very recently, even the British did not attempt to impose a new structure of society on the Indians but, on the other hand, they had deliberately adopted the local institutions to suit their needs in order, of course, to further their interests. [In this context, it is worth while and interesting to note that the modern "study of the ancient Indian social order owed its inception to the policy of the East India Company, which could not govern an alien people without some knowledge of their institutions. The preface to *A Code of Gentoo Laws* (London, 1776), one of the first English works which have some bearing on the early social history of India, states that 'the importance of the commerce of India and the advantages of a territorial establishment in Bengal' could be maintained only by 'an adoption of such ori-ginal institutions of the country as do not intimately clash with the laws or interests of the conquerors'... In his preface to the translation of the *Manu Smṛiti* (Calcutta, 1794), Sir William Jones, the father of modern Indology, adds that if this policy is pursued, 'the well-directed industry of many millions of Hindu subjects . . . would largely add to the wealth of Britain' . . . after the mutiny, and especially from about the end of the nineteenth century, it was felt necessary by many members of the adminis-tration to stress divisions of caste, race, language, etc. as a shield against the growing nationalist demands. . ."[166]].

Thus, in this matter of the retention of the various socio-cultural levels in India, we can eliminate such possibilities as the biological extinction or dispersion of the Harappans into obscurity, or the absorption of the native (Harappan) society into the conquering (Aryan) 'hordes', or even that of war of all (non-Aryans) against all (Aryans) until extinction.[167] Therefore, one cannot seriously believe the Aryan texts of the physical extinction of all the pre-Aryans, or logically see the 'disappearance' and 'destruction' of most of the population of Harappan society. It may, of course, be surmised that the Aryans employed some sort of hit-and-run tactics, which nomadic pastoralists often do utilize, with brief attacks on fields, dams, etc., on which the peasant-urban Harappan systems had depended. The effect of this form of contact with a technologically superior and very different cultural group would be to throw the indigenous Harappan peasant-urban integration and social organization into disarray and, thereby, render the internal arrangements of the urban areas ineffective. This disarray is seen in the archaeological evidence of the last levels which, in turn, may have caused refugee movements from the urban areas to the south and east of the Indus. But this movement would also decidedly imply the transmission and continuance of the Harappan ideology, and their socio-cultural systems. Of course, this Aryan contact may not have been the major cause of Harappan 'disintegration', but it may well have been the 'triggering off' device that started the spread and abandonment of the Harappans from the Indus basin, because it probably had already begun due to 'environmental' reasons and the other inherent causes of maintaining the integration of the expanding peasant-urban system.

At any rate, the Harappan population could not have simply disappeared even if there was a major aggressive meeting of the two 'cultures' which at present is not really seen in any archaeological evidence. But even such a meeting implies the gradual assimilation and interchange, or acculturation, which is always a two-way process. The actual details of this process have to be worked out, but it may be recalled that the Aryan nomads were not equipped with an organization that would fit a sedentary life, in order to start a peasant-urban 'civilization' *de novo*. Therefore, what probably may have happened is that the Aryan superstructure of ideology was imposed upon the old socio-economic organization, and this was then gradually formalized and incorporated into the sacred texts of the Aryans. Hence, it was, contrary to the general opinion, not the Aryanization of India but rather the Indianization of the Aryan nomadic pastoralist hordes. Let us look at this significant process a little more closely, as follows:

The process that resulted in some form of an integrated system of the Indian Style may be visualized as the acculturation of two societies which, by and large, had certain basic similarities even though their cultural superstructure, perhaps, showed great diversities. What this means is that most probably both these societies were employing equally advanced techniques of agriculture and metallurgy, with some form of class divisions etc., yet they varied in their crops, gods, artistic production, literature and in many other ways. Therefore, the culture-contact situations of these two 'cultures' may be considered in terms of the contact of two antagonistic 'societies', and even if this contact had been a violent one, in this situation the populations would have stabilized after a while because the invaders could not possibly have exterminated the natives. What seems plausible is that it was more a case of the Aryans merely taking over the upper ranks of the hierarchy of the non-Aryans. The Aryans would now have collected 'taxes' etc. and even taken care—as the ceramic and other evidences suggest—to maintain the specialized craftsmen, peasantry, etc., albeit suited to their style. Thus, with the passage of time, a more temperate process of diffusion would have been set to work which 'diluted' both the cultures, and for the time being created a somewhat anomalous society. This process of acculturation implies the influx of strange words into each other's language and vocabulary; it also means the emergence of new gods and other cultural items and traits. These latter 'facts' of acculturation are clearly demonstrated by archaeological and textual evidence. The acculturative types and determinants, etc. of this form of acculturation process are clearly illustrated and discussed in social science literature. Hence, it is in the light of this process that one sees, even today, in existence numerous (to the extent of 40 per cent) non-Aryan deities, ceremonies and rituals in the villages of the region that was known as the heart of the *Āryāvarta*.[168] This and many other facts once more exemplify that the ideal values so often characterized in Indian classical and sacred literature are quite at variance with the actual or 'real' beliefs and values that persist within the basic socio-economic pattern of Indian society.

Similarly, it is within the laws and generalizations of the social sciences that the disappearance and re-emergence of urbanization in India could perhaps also be explained. This so-called 'second' urbanization of India has generally been attributed to Western influences such as the coming of Alexander the Great, Bactrian kings or Vitruvius, and the Romans, etc.[169] But this seems less likely in the light of what has been stated in this chapter, and also because there was not enough time to intervene between Alexander and the 'historical' cities such as Pāṭaliputra, whose description by Megasthenes reminds one of Harappa and Mohenjodaro.[170] Moreover, the great elaboration of Indian thought, specially that which is found in the various treatises on art and architecture, must have required many many years of development and formation, and it could not have been the overnight creation due to Greek, Persian or Roman ideas. There is no doubt that the typical Harappan urban areas of the Indus basin had disappeared in the 'disorder' that followed. But, as has been stressed, the institutions, ideas, etc.—the ideology and structure of Harappan society—did not 'disappear' everywhere. However, town planning and urbanization are associated with some form of centralized 'power' or 'authority', as well as with trade and commerce. Therefore, while the older structure and organization were in disarray, with the coming of the Aryans and many other causes, urban areas could only have reappeared with a new stability of the socio-cultural-economic organization and order of society, i.e., until some equilibrium was re-established. In the meantime, of course, other factors were also influencing and affecting Indian society, such as the crucial fact of the introduction of the plough and iron metallurgy, etc. Consequently, this meant the introduction of new socio-economic systems which involved a readjustment and reorganization of society.

In other words, in the later phases of the Formative Period may be seen a 'transitional' society, from what was to emerge, fully, the Indian Style. Thus, it was not until the re-emergence of a social order by readjustment, and the re-formulation and stabilization of ideas, beliefs, etc., that a centralized 'authority' could re-emerge. This must only then have resulted in the re-emergence of urban areas which, as we know, show clear resemblance to the basic planned pattern of the older Harappan urban areas albeit with many new foreign elements in it.[171]

NOTES AND REFERENCES

1. Malinowski, B., *Scientific Theory of Culture*, 1960, p. 49.
2. Childe, V. G., "The Urban Revolution", *Town Planning Review*, 21, 1950, pp. 3-17.
3. Kroeber, A. L., *An Anthropologist Looks at History*, University of California, Berkley, 1963, pp. v, 4, 5, 17, 20.
4. Lehman, F. K., "Typology and the Classification of Socio-Cultural Systems", *Process and Pattern in Culture*, ed. Robert A. Manners, Aldine, Chicago, 1964, p. 393.
5. Redfield, Robert, *The Primitive World and its Transformation*, New York, 1962, pp. 51-52.
6. Redfield, Robert, *Peasant Society and Culture*, Chicago, 1963.
7. Marriott, Mckim, "Little Communities in an Indigenous Civilization", *Village India*, ed. Marriott, Chicago, 1955, p. 181.

8. Firth, Raymond, *Elements of Social Organization*, Boston, 1961, p. 42.

9. Kant, Edgar, "Classification and Problems of Migration", *Readings in Cultural Geography*, eds. Philip C. Wagner and Marvin D. Mikesell, Chicago, 1962, pp. 344.

10. Radcliffe-Brown, A. R., *Structure and Function in Primitive Society*, Cohen and West, 1964, p. 12.

11. Ibid., p. 180.

12. Rao, S. R., in *Indian Prehistory — 1964*, eds. Misra and Mate, 1965, p. 130.

13. Service, Elman R., *Primitive Social Organzation*, 1964, p. 199.

14. Radcliffe-Brown, A. R., op. cit., 1964, pp. 4-5.

15. Ibid., p. 10.

16. Ibid., pp. 10, 43.

17. Ibid., p. 11.

18. Radcliffe-Brown, A. R., *A Natural Science of Society*, Glencoe, 1964, p. 80.

19. Ibid., pp. 121, 128.

20. Redfield, Robert, *The Little Community*, Chicago, 1963, p. 91.

21. Ibid., *Peasant Society and Culture*, Chicago, 1963, p. 45.

22. Ibid., pp. 40-41.

23. Ibid., *Introducing India*, Singer, Chicago, 1957, p. 14.

24. Ibid., 1963.

25. Ibid., "The Folk Society", *American Journal of Sociology*, Vol. 52, January 1947, p. 293.

26. Foster, George M., " What is Folk Culture", *American Anthropologist*, Vol. 55, 1953, pp. 159-173.

27. Redfield, Robert, *Peasant Society and Culture*, 1963, pp. 18-19.

28. Ibid.

29. Sjoberg, Gideon, "The Preindustrial City", *American Journal of Sociology*, Vol. LX, 1955, pp. 438-445.

30. Redfield, Robert, *Peasant Society and Culture*, 1963, pp. 30-34.

31. Ibid., pp. 41-42.

32. Service, Elman R., op. cit., quoted, 1964, p. vii.

33. Marriott, Mckim, in op. cit., 1955, pp. 186-187.

34. Braidwood, Robert J. and Linda; A rejoinder to Julian Steward's "Cultural Causality and Law: A Trial Formulation of the Development of Early Civilizations", *American Anthropologist*, 51, 1949, pp. 665-669.

35. Lal, B. B., in *Ancient India* 18-19, New Delhi, 1962-63, pp. 208-221.

36. Marshall, John, *Mohenjodaro and Indus Civilization*, Vols. I & II, 1937.

37. Mackay, E. J. H., *Further Excavations at Mohenjodaro*, Vols. I & II, 1937-38; and *Chanhudaro Excavations*, New Delhi, 1943.

38. Piggot, S., *Prehistoric India*, Pelican, 1950.

39. Childe, V. G., *New Light on the Most Ancient East*, London, 1954.

40. Wheeler, R. E. M., *The Indus Civilization*, Cambridge, 1953; *Early India and Pakistan*, London, 1959; *Civilizations of Indus Valley and Beyond*, London, 1966.
41. Wheeler, ibid., 1959, pp. 108-109.
42. Wheeler, ibid., 1953, pp. 58-59.
43. Sankalia, *Prehistory and Protohistory in India and Pakistan*, 1962, pp. 155-156.
44. Rao, S. R., in *Ancient India* 18-19, New Delhi, 1962-63, pp. 5-207.
45. Dhaky, M. A., in Misra, op. cit., 1965, pp. 124-127.
46. Ghosh, A., ibid., p. 115.
47. Ibid.
48. Ibid.
49. Fairservis, Walter A., *Archaeological Surveys in Zhob and Loralai Districts, West Pakistan*, American Museum Natural History, Vol. 47, part 2, 1959, pp. 273-448.
50. Sharma, Y. D., in Misra, op. cit., 1965, p. 134.
51. Sarkar, S. S., *Ancient Races of Baluchistan, Panjab and Sind*, Bookland, 1964.
52. Rao, S. R., in Misra, op. cit., 1965, p. 130.
53. Ghosh, A., ibid., p. 123.
54. Ibid., p. 124.
55. Sharma, Y. D., ibid., p. 134.
56. Deshpande, M. N., ibid., p. 128.
57. Ibid.
58. Ibid., pp. 127-128.
59. Gour, R. C., ibid., p. 142.
60. Misra, V. N., ibid., pp. 147-148.
61. Wankanker, V. S., ibid., p. 149.
62. Bannerjee, N. R., ibid., p. 191.
63. Ibid.
64. Ibid.
65. Ibid.
66. Ibid.
67. Sankalia, H. D., "New Light on the 'Aryan' Invasion of India: Links discovered in Central India with Iran of 1000 B.C.", *Illustrated London News*, September 20, 1958, pp. 478-479.
68. Subbarao, B., "The Chalcolithic Blade Industries of Maheshwar and a Note on the History of the Technique", *Bulletin of the Deccan College Research Institute*, Vol. XVII, No. 2, Poona, 1955, pp. 126-149.
69. Allchin, F. R., *Neolithic Cattle Keepers of South India*, Cambridge, 1963.
70. Ibid.
71. Subbarao, B., *Personality of India*, 1958, pp. 83-84.
72. Gupta, S. P., in Misra, op. cit., 1965, p. 100.

73. Soundara Rajan, K. V., ibid., p. 106.

74. Ghosh, A., ibid., p. 99.

75. Childe, V. G., *Man Makes Himself*, Mentor, 1957.

76. Harris, Marvin, "The Economy has No Surplus ?", *American Anthropologist*, 61, 1959, pp. 185-199.

77. Ibid.

78. Kosambi, D. D., *The Culture and Civilization of Ancient India in Historical Outline*, London, 1965, p. 62.

79. Fairservis, Walter A., "The Harappan Civilization — New Evidence and More Theory", *American Museum Novitates*, No. 2055, 17, 1961, p. 15.

80. Wheeler, op. cit., 1953, pp. 37, 40, 92.

81. Fairservis, in op. cit., 1961; in op. cit., No. 2302, 1967.

82. Adams, Robert M., "Early Civilization, Subsistence, and Environment", in *City Invincible*, eds. Kraeling and Adams, Chicago, 1960, pp. 269-294.

83. Stanislawski, Dan, "The Origin and Spread of the Grid Pattern Town", in Wagner and Mikesell, op. cit., Chicago, 1962, pp. 318-329.

84. Service, op. cit., 1964, p. 172.

85. Arendt, Hannah, in ibid., p. 160.

86. Bennet, John W. and Tumin, Melvin M., "Some Cultural Imperatives", in Peter Hammond, op. cit., 1964, pp. 9-21.

87. Ibid., p. 16.

88. Service, op. cit., 1964, pp. 27-28.

89. Ibid., p. 181.

90. Ibid., p. 173.

91. Ibid., pp. 144-145.

92. Ibid., p. 161.

93. Sharma, R. S., *Light on Early Indian Society and Economy*, 1966, p. 5.

94. Ibid.

95. Berreman, Gerald D., "Caste in India and the United States", *American Journal of Sociology*, Vol. LXVI, 1960, pp. 120-127; and Leach, E. R. ed., *Caste in South India, Ceylon and North-West Pakistan*, Cambridge, 1962.

96. Gough, Kathleen, in Leach, ibid., pp. 11-60.

97. Kosambi, op. cit., 1965, p. 78.

98. Redfield, op. cit., 1962, p. 36.

99. Thapar, in Misra, op. cit., 1965, p. 160.

100. Wheeler, op. cit., 1953, p. 64.

101. Fairservis, Walter A., "Problems in Post-Harappan Archaeology in the Lower Indus Valley and Baluchistan", Special *Subbarao Memorial Number of Maharaja Sayajirao University of Baroda*, Vol. XV, 1 1967, pp. 25-36.

102. Redfield, op. cit., 1962, p. 57.

103. Ibid., p. 65.

104. Ibid., p. 41.

105. Service, op. cit., 1964, p. 166.

106. Redfield, op. cit., 1962, p. 34.

107. Ibid.

108. Ibid., p. 177.

109. Sarkar, op. cit., 1964, pp. 13-15.

110. Kosambi, op cit., 1965; Wheeler op. cit., 1959; Piggot, op. cit., 1950, etc.

111. Wheeler, op. cit., 1953, 1959.

112. Piggot, op. cit., 1950.

113. Fairservis, in op. cit., 1966, 1967.

114. Adams, Robert M., "Agriculture and Urban Life in Early South-Western Iran", *New Roads to Yesterday*, ed. Joseph R. Caldwell, 1966, pp. 436-465; and Adams and Thorkild Jacobsen, "Salt and Silt in Ancient Mesopotamian Agriculture", ibid., Basic Books, New York, pp. 446-479.

115. Raikes, Robert L. and Dyson, R. H., "The Prehistoric Climate of Baluchistan and the Indus Valley", *American Anthropologist*, 63, 2, 1961, pp. 265-281; and Raikes, "The End of the Ancient Cities of the Indus Civilization in Sind and Baluchistan", *Am. Anth.*, 65, 3, 1963, pp. 655-659; Fairservis, in op. cit., 1967.

116. Rao, S. R., in *Ancient India*, 1962-63.

117. Wheeler, op cit., 1953, p. 91.

118. Childe, op. cit., 1954, p. 184.

119. Ibid.

120. Ibid.

121. Lal, B. B., "A New Indus Valley Provincial Capital Discovered: Excavations at Kalibangan in Northern Rajasthan", *Illustrated London News*, March 1962, pp. 454-457.

122. Childe, op. cit., 1954, p. 184.

123. Ibid., pp. 184-185.

124. Wheeler, op. cit., 1953, p. 61.

125. Allchin, op. cit., 1963, pp. 119, 124, 126.

126. Fairservis, in op. cit., 1961, p. 30.

127. Misra, op. cit., 1965, p. 153.

128. Gour, ibid., p. 145.

129. Rao, ibid., pp. 129-130.

130. Thapar, ibid., p. 161.

131. Bannerjee, N. R., ibid., p. 141.

132. Ibid.

133. Lal, B. B., in *Ancient India* 10 & 11, 1954-55; Bannerjee, N. R., *The Iron Age in India*, Delhi, 1965.

134. Deshpande, M. N., in Misra, op. cit., 1965, p. 129.

135. Gour, ibid., p. 144.
136. Sharma, R. S., op. cit., 1966, p. 56.
137. Ibid., p. 58.
138. Ibid.
139. Ibid., p. 56.
140. Ibid., p. 57.
141. Ibid., p. 58.
142. Kosambi, op. cit., 1965, p. 80.
143. Ibid., p. 124.
144. Ibid., p. 125.
145. Ray, Amita, *Villages, Towns and Secular Buildings in Ancient India,* Calcutta, 1963, p. 47.
146. Ibid.
147. Kosambi, op. cit., 1965, p. 71.
148. Ray, Amita, op. cit., 1963.
149. Sharma, R. S., op. cit., 1966, p. 55.
150. Ray, Amita, op. cit., 1963.
151. Ibid., pp. 47-48.
152. Ibid.
153. Ibid., p. 49.
154. Ibid., p. 50.
155. Ibid., p. 71.
156. Ibid., p. 110.
157. Sharma, R. S., op. cit., 1966, p. 90.
158. Ibid., p. 94.
159. Kosambi, op. cit., 1965, pp. 81-83.
160. Wheeler, op. cit., 1953, p. 69.
161. Kosambi, op. cit., 1965, pp. 114-118.
162. Wheeler, op. cit., 1953, p. 95.
163. Childe, op. cit., 1954, p. 183-185.
164. Fairservis, in op. cit., 1961, p. 33.
165. Fried, Morton H., "Land Tenure, Geography and Ecology in Contact of Cultures", *American Journal of Economics and Sociology,* Vol. 11, July 1952., pp. 391-412.
166. Sharma, R. S., op. cit., 1966, p. 1.
167. Aberle, David F. and others, "The Functional Prerequisites of a Society", *Ethics,* Vol. 60, 1950, pp. 100-111.
168. Marriott, in op. cit., 1955, pp. 209-210.
169. Stanislawski, in Wagner and Mikesell, op. cit., 1962, p. 322.
170. Basham, A. L., *The Wonder that was India,* London, 1965.
171. Ray, Amita, op. cit., 1963.

CULTURE AREAS, REGIONALISM
AND ARCHAEOLOGY

In the earlier part of the previous chapter we had mentioned that the all-India process of Indianization is only one set of the two concrescent processes which have gone into the making of Indian civilization and its Style, i.e., this all-India process of the formation of systems and institutions is intimately inter-woven, to complicate matters, with the inevitable second Indian theme of regional process or 'diversity' and with which we shall be concerned here. Hence, it is quite normal to hear the oft-repeated slogan of 'unity in diversity'. However, there has been, in public affairs, in general a strong tendency to lay emphasis on the unitary aspect of India. There are, of course, both older traditional and modern political reasons why in public affairs 'unity' rather than 'diversity' is stressed. But the social and political scientists, art-historians, archaeologists, etc. have an equally strong tendency for making broad generalizations in the unitary sense as if the personality of India is one unit either 'geographically' or as a socio-cultural entity. Somehow, one of the very obvious fundamental facts which are often overlooked is that the subcontinent is as large as Europe (excluding European USSR) and it has even a broader spectrum of environ-mental situation than is the case in Europe. The effects of this complex mosaic of the environmental situation of the subconti-nent on India's cultural history, and the consequent cultural mosaic are extremely relevant for understanding many aspects of India's past or present complex civilization. However, this concern with 'environment' is not a reference to the role of geographic factors in history because the concern of this chapter is to elaborate on this important theme of 'diversity'

and, specially, to establish certain 'viable' Culture Areas
(a concept that has been borrowed from among the many
concepts of Cultural Ecology) with reference to the archaeological evidence of the Formative Period. This approach will,
incidentally, also illustrate that archaeology can, and must,
relate its subject-matter to the problems of the contemporary
situation. Moreover, it will indicate the fact that men of public
affairs—and many others besides—cannot afford to ignore the
depth of culture-history. But before proceeding on to the main
theme, the following is a summary of the concepts of Cultural
Ecology (which should form a part of the post-graduate syllabi
of archaeology in India).

Ecology has been defined as the action aspect of geography
that "combines indigenous resources with a specific cultural
inventory of exploitative techniques, making possible a certain
distribution of human population over a particular region".[1]
In very general terms, the ecological complex covers the four
main referential concepts of population, environment, technology and social organization, i.e., it devotes itself to the problems of the habitat of cultural communities of every stage and
condition. But many of its concepts which are today employed
in the studies of human populations are, in fact, borrowed from
biological ecology. Among the analytical tools which ecology
uses in investigating the intricate ties between man and his
external surroundings are such constructs as the eco-system,
ecological niche, community and equilibrium, etc. In anthropology, ecological analysis has been commonly employed to understand the relations of socio-cultural systems to their external
environments. This broad form of inquiry has come to be
known as Cultural Ecology, but as a means of analysis it neither
possesses any particular intrinsic category of data nor does it
rest on a unity of theoretical foundations.[2] However, one of
the important concepts included in it is that of the eco-system
which deals with the problems of the relation of one system to

another, such as the structure of the system, its function and what the mechanisms of articulation between the eco-system and the social system are. This concept has been found very useful as a framework for archaeological research in the Euro-American context, and it will be useful for Indian archaeology as well. But the ecological approach should not be confused with the old problem of a concern to seek a solution to the relationship of environment to culture in terms of the one-to-one approach which presumes a static interaction of man with his environment. On the contrary, this interaction, according to the ecological approach, is in continuous change because of the variations in environmental features, population dynamics, social institutions, etc., and the adaptive quality of culture which is characteristic of all human societies. Therefore the concept of Cultural Ecology is very useful, that is, because its concern is with the *process* implied in the *sequence* of culture-historical events. Moreover, it is within Cultural Ecology that the concept of Culture Areas (or Cultural Landscapes) is also included. Culture Areas have been defined as territories which are inhabited at any given period of time by human communities characterized by particular cultures.[3] "A culture-area, in geographic terms constitutes a 'region'. . . The culture-area then is an assemblage of such forms as have interdependence and is functionally differentiated from other areas".[4] Thus, it is within the briefly stated concepts of Cultural Ecology and Culture Areas that the problem of the beginnings of the process of 'diversity' in the Indian Style shall now be discussed.

The problem of delimiting the various 'regions' of India has quite often been discussed in archaeology, anthropology, history, etc. But many of these delimitations, specially in archaeology, have by and large been intellectual abstractions, in the sense that these are generally derived from classifications more suited to geographical research, or else are arbitrary divisions which are based on a single criterion. The commonmost classification that archaeologists have used is generally the one which has been borrowed from the landscape classifications of geography, such as the geomorphological divisions of the subcontinent into the three primary areas of the Himalayan uplands, the Indo-Gangetic plains and Peninsular India along with their various secondary and tertiary subdivisions. The other abstract divisions which are used are the ones that are based on the river systems like the Indus, Ganges, Narmada, Tapti, etc.[5] But, obviously, the latter too are of little value since rivers pass through varied ecological, climatic and cultural zones. These and the other devices for classifying archaeological relics in their geographical setting are, therefore, not worth-while for any meaningful understanding of either the past or the present cultural processes because they do not enable us to establish 'functional' regions as viable Culture Areas.

The regional divisions of India, as followed by archaeologists, have seldom been based on any 'functional' concept such as the one of Culture Areas in which the "spatial content furnishes a convenient invariant set of reference points for observation, and the observed spatio-temporal regularities and rhythms furnish convenient indications of the structural relationships".[6] There is, however, an exception in the late Prof. B. Subbarao[7] who had used Spate's[8] classification of 'regions', based on soil and climatic factors and which takes into consideration such differentiating features as forest cover, aridity, etc. But Prof. Subbarao was oriented in the historical tradition and, therefore, had used Spate's classification to explain certain questions of historiography, such as the spread and movements of peoples and cultures as well as the differential technological development of the various regions as are seen in India's early culture-history. Subbarao's approach was adequate for his own frame of reference, but it seems inadequate for the topic of the present chapter on the diversity of India. In any case, Subbarao was the first archaeologist in India who seems to have used some kind of a conceptual scheme—albeit a historio-geographical one—in order to explain India's early culture-history.

The great importance of the ecological approach to the study of archaeological problems had also been stressed by the late Prof. V. Gordon Childe in these words: "A deeper analysis and ecological description of recognized cultures directed towards disclosing the functional integration of their surviving constitutions and reconstituting the economic and sociological linkages between the latter are suitable themes for doctoral theses".[9] Similarly, Prof. Grahme Clark has stated that one "of the principal attractions of prehistory is the opportunity it offers for studying the interplay of social aspirations and environing nature over long periods of time".[10] In India, often, as may be seen in the archaeological reports, the ecological or the environmental approach seems to have been construed to mean the narrower preoccupation of simply identifying and listing the flora and fauna and the raw material of the finds discovered during archaeological explorations and excavations. This method and procedure is of little use by itself unless certain processual interpretations are also made from the study and identifications of the materials recovered. To take a case in point, Prof. Braidwood[11] has shown the great relevance of the ecological approach for West Asia both in archaeology and ethnology, and one which enabled him to infer and deduce the differences of the contrasting prehistoric environments, such as between a seashore or inland, hill country versus flood-plains, etc. In following the cultural ecological approach Prof. Braidwood's procedure was to analyse the ancient sites within their immediate surroundings, that is, analyse the micro-environment or what might be called the smaller subdivisions of the larger ecological zones.

However, the problem of establishing certain processual correlations between environment and culture, specially during the prehistoric periods within this framework of the ecological concept, is neither a simple one nor is it ever possible for it to be conclusive. And the reason ? Because, primarily, it involves the difficult and hazardous task of establishing the palaeoclimate of a given region. Therefore, it is only in those cases where the local conditions have not changed substantially between the prehistoric periods investigated and those of the present that such modes of analysis for purposes of establishing Culture Areas would be worth while to attempt. Moreover, any correlations or generalizations with regard to 'culture and environment' which may be suggested are further complicated by the fact, as one learns from the vast number of ethnographic instances, that there are different cultures which have similar subsistence patterns or have comparable general features and yet these have been found to occupy different environments. Conversely, it has been seen that there are instances of areas which have similar environments and yet these have reared up human societies that seem to differ a great deal in their cultural content. Nevertheless, in very general terms, it has been established that there is a close interrelationship between 'Man and Environment' or 'natural' regions and cultures. The problem that now remains is one of working out detailed specific examples in order to illustrate this approach in the case of India. Any elaboration of this problem on the basis of fieldwork is beyond the scope of the present monograph. We will only be able to indicate the usefulness of the Culture Area concept as a heuristic device for students of Indian society, culture and civilization.

In order, therefore, to establish certain Culture Areas, the first problem was to find a more relevant classification of 'regions' of the Indian subcontinent than had hitherto been used either by the archaeologist or the historian. The broad categories of the macro-regions of the classification, which are used in this section, have been constructed by geographers who have drawn upon the combined knowledge of the physical divisions, climate and soil classifications of India. But this combined knowledge has been worked out within certain statistical concepts that has enabled the geographers to form a composite picture of the regions and the distribution of weather elements. These concepts are primarily based on such factors which contribute to the growth of a statistical or average climatic model within a specified boundary as it is revealed in climo-statical characteristics from region to region.[12] The elements mentioned in these studies have been modified from the well-known Koeppen and Thornwaite's systems which include, thermal conditions, precipitation conditions, native vegetation, the nature of the upper wind, land in relation to depression, and the monthly and seasonal percentage distribution of any climatic element. These well-known systems of classifications have also used some of the fundamentals of climatic classification such as clouds, humidity and precipitation, temperature and equirange zone classification, and the characteristic graph of the distribution of climatic elements.[13] It has been observed that the various general climatic types recur in several areas of India as a result of the large measure of recurrence of somewhat similar elements and conditions such as, for example, tropical rain forests occur in Eastern India as well as along the Western Konkan coast. It should, similarly, be borne in mind that in nature there are never any sharp discontinuities between the different zones but there are only gradations.

In short, an acceptable classification of the regions of present-day India was found which is based on the statistical treatment of the weather elements as they have been correlated to soil factors and the physical divisions of India.[14] This classification was found to be equally relevant for the Formative Period (proto-historic) evidence because it is generally accepted nowadays that earth's climate has not changed greatly since the end of the Pleistocene Period, i.e., not enough to substantially alter the basic ecological zones. However, the ecological boundaries must have fluctuated but more, perhaps, because of the agency of man than by 'nature'. Therefore, this classification may also possibly be found to be of some relevance for establishing palaeo-climatic regions of India during the Pleistocene Period, but it will require very detailed work. Thus, the following is the classification of the regions (Fig. 6):

Major Regions	*Sub-regions*
1. Himalayas	A. Western Himalayas
	B. Eastern Himalayas
	C. Brahmaputra Valley
	D. Assam Highlands
2. Northern Plains	A. Lower Gangetic Plain
	B. Middle Gangetic Plain
	C. Upper Gangetic Plain
	D. Trans-Gangetic Plain
	E. Rajasthan Desert
3. Peninsular Hills and Plateau	A. North-west Hills
	B. North-central Hills
	C. North-east Plateau
	D. North Deccan
	E. South Deccan
4. Western Ghats and Coast	A. Gujarat
	B. Konkan Coast
	C. Malabar Coast
5. Eastern Ghats and Coast	A. Tamilnad
	B. Andhra-Orissa Coast

The next step carried out was to ascertain whether these 'natural' regions were coincidental with Culture Areas. Therefore, upon this map of the 'natural' regions was superimposed the known approximate distribution map of the major groups

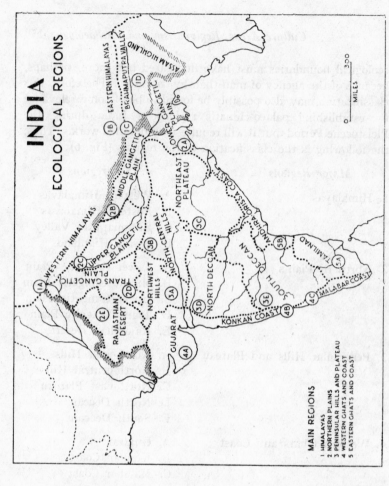

Fig. 6. *India — Natural
Regions*

of the various archaeological 'cultures' of the Formative Period. This superimposition revealed that there was a fairly neat—though approximate—coincidence of the cultural boundaries with the regional boundaries. It further indicated that the 'natural' regions were closely related to India's early culture history, and that these 'natural' areas thus seem to have been transformed into Culture Areas (Fig. 7). It will be noticed from this map that there are certain areas which show an unclear correlation or are simply blank ones, such as the Indo-Gangetic plain, areas of Orissa, etc. The reason for this, most probably, is the lack of insufficient archaeological data for these areas.

In any case, the interrelationship of 'environment' to socio-economic organization and the settlement pattern etc. of the early human communities is fairly well known. This is so because in India, as well as elsewhere in the world, various studies have shown the close correlation between certain geological formations and the economic pattern of human communities. For instance, in the Western India of today, one observes that the trappean fertile black soil is the land of wheat and cotton, whereas the area of the metamorphic loams in Andhra is more suitable for the cultivation of rice, sugar, sesamum and millet. Again, Telangana is a land of tanks and other artificial means of irrigation because it has a soil that cannot retain moisture even though it has a better but uncertain rainfall.[15] Now, bearing in mind these differences in the two areas today, it has been shown that this difference in these two ecological areas is also reflected in the archaeological evidence of the earliest sedentary food-producing extensive settlements of both the areas. Thus, the upper reaches of the Godavari were exploited by the 'Chalcolithic' communities which nad employed heavy metal tools of copper and bronze in order to clear the dense forests while, on the other hand, the 'neolithic' agricultural communities along the lower reaches of the

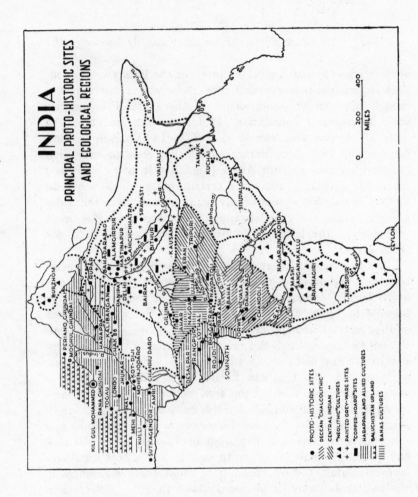

Fig. 7.
India — Early
Culture Areas

162

Godavari lived by stone-tool technology in settlements which were located on or near the hills of outcrops overlooking their fields. These 'neolithic' communities had depended on basalt and diorite for their stone tools which was only obtainable from these very hills.[16] Consequently, the settlement pattern of the early archaeological cultures in the different regions of India was governed by certain 'environmental' factors.

At any rate, we also know from other evidences that these Culture Areas are viable ones. For instance, it has been mentioned in the previous chapter that there is regional continuity from the Formative Period even until today in the various Culture Areas of India such as in certain traits and traditions as well as in the population composition of the physical human types. Some detailed research to show this continuity of the regional pattern from the remote past into the present has been recently carried out, specially for the Deccan.[17] The latter work suggests that the Deccan 'neolithic' culture shows continuity into the present-day 'cultures' of the region. This study was carried out within the integrative interdisciplinary approach of examining not only the archaeological evidence but also the current place-names, the local cattle-sites and the other traditions of the ash-mounds, cattle-ponds, etc.

It is clear that there has been a long thread of continuity in the socio-cultural and socio-economic patterns within the various regions of India. However, this continuity cannot be seen by employing the traditional approach of building up archaeological sequences of 'cultural' succession because, to repeat, this conceptual framework is not explanatory. Accordingly, these sequences are merely convenient subdivisions of an historical continuum. Moreover, the common interpretation of these successions is that one 'culture' complex replaces and obliterates another. But this, as has been mentioned in the previous chapter, is the 19th century typological concept of evolution since it ignores the fact that new cultural complexes and traits are added on, at least in the case of India, to the old ones. Of course, eventually, new patterns do emerge, but there remain in them the older elements that are never suddenly replaced or obliterated. In India, especially, the gradual development of the cultural forms seems not only to be obvious but the rule. Thus, regional cultural continuities here will only be seen in terms of what might be called the genetic explanations of historical phenomena, or the cultural-ecological and the processual explanation. For instance, from this processual viewpoint it will be seen that the problem debated currently of 'regionalism', 'linguism', etc. in India is not only obviously the result of recent history but also the fruit of even farther past complex processes, that is, many of the complex cultural phenomena of India cannot be explained without referring to the long evolutionary processes that have been going on in the regions of India, very possibly from the remote 'neolithic' times and the ecological complex around which human groups are organized.

In any case, there is a clear indication that the significant early culture-historical diversities of the subcontinent suggest an obvious fundamental interaction with the 'natural' regions. In the absence of detailed archaeological data for the Formative Period, further correlations of the 'environment' to 'culture' for this period were not possible except in a very generalized manner as has been briefly stated above. Therefore, in order to provide further proof of the validity of the Culture Area concept and to show the probable long continuity of India's regions, the next best step that seemed to be was to borrow the familiar principle of historical research, which is to proceed from the known to the unknown.

II

The political map of India, in recent years, has been reorganized on the linguistic basis.[18] The States Reorganization

Commission had very briefly dealt with the various 'cultural' factors while demarcating the new states within their linguistic boundaries. However, it is fairly well known that anthropologists have also used language more often than any other element of culture to delimit Culture Areas because any developed language, along with its close associates of exclamations, gestures, facial expressions, etc., is an essential medium of human communication and, therefore, is a critical component of its cultural setting. It is within this framework of the close association of language and culture that the setting up of India's present linguistic states has to be viewed and understood because the linguistic and the consequent relative cultural homogeneity is typical of each state or region. Of course, this statement does not contradict our previous statement that there are also marked fundamental similarities in the socio-cultural institutions and features of Indian Style that are prevalent in each region, which freely cut across the diverse areas.

Consequently, bearing in mind the close relationship of language, culture and society, upon the 'natural' regions map was, once again, superimposed the recently reorganized politico-linguistic map of India. This superimposition revealed that the state boundaries of the 'new' Indian states coincided even neater—although still approximately—with the boundaries of the 'natural' regions than had been the case previously (Fig. 8). Hence, there was a clear suggestion that the political states of reorganized India reflected rather closely, even today, not only the cultural but also the main 'natural' regions of the Indian subcontinent. This process, as has been hinted at before, most probably began with the Formative Period with the early socio-cultural differentiation of the 'natural' regions. Therefore, there is every likelihood that the present linguistic states are, generally speaking, historically old and persisting Culture Areas. However, from the point of political history these areas have also been classified as stable and semi-stable 'core' areas (Fig. 9).

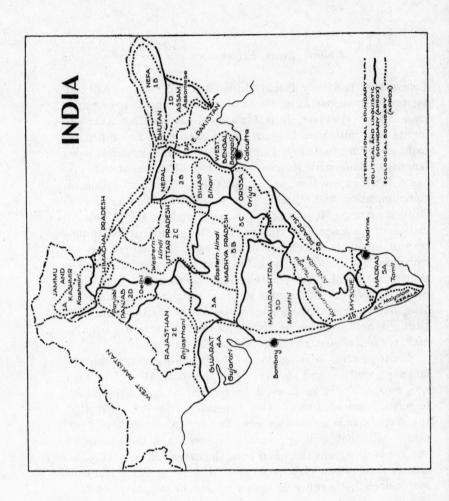

Fig. 8.
India — Natural
Regions and
State Boundaries

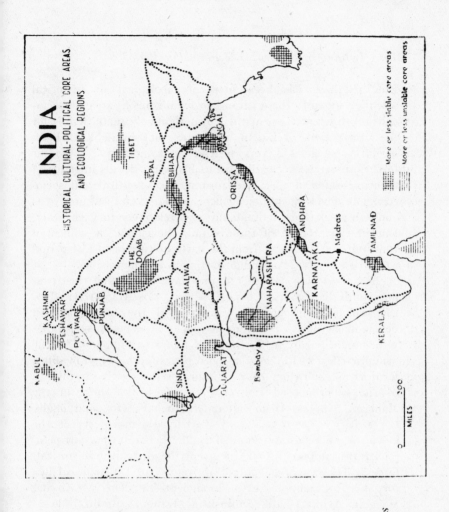

Fig. 9.
India — Regions
and Political
Core Areas

But as there has been little archaeological or historical attention given to these various regional cores as areas of socio-cultural differentiation in their own right, adequate details for the later periods of Indian history are not available. There-fore, this suggests a very fruitful and imperative topic for further research which will give us historical details in terms of the time rates of the socio-cultural, socio-political and socio-economic developmental sequences in the several Culture Areas and sub-areas, both individually and relatively to each other. But in the absence of these details, developing a sequential continuity of our theme from the early culture-historical period to the later periods of Indian history was not possible.

Nevertheless, some other studies have shown that the dyna-mics of Indian political history is very closely interrelated to the ecological (geographical) process of the formation and development of these Culture Areas. These pertinent studies were carried out by Y. A. Raikar,[19] following Subbarao.[20] The synoptic chart of Raikar's has been presented here in a modified form as a graph (Fig. 10). It indicates the relative instability of the superimposed centralized empires like those of the Mauryan, Guptas, Delhi-Sultanate, Mughals, etc., and finally the British. These relatively short-lived empires reflect the inevitable and constant political conflict between the centripetal (politically imposed) and the centrifugal (culture-historical) forces. The centrifugal forces are represented in political his-tory by the examples of such ancient kingdoms as Kosala, Magadh, Avanti, Lāta, Saurashtra, Kalinga, Andhra, Maha-rashtra, Karnatak, Chera, Chola, Pāṇdya, etc. This apparent political conflict between the centripetal and centrifugal forces which has very often been over-emphasised by our political historians is in fact symptomatic of the underlying strong cul-ture-historical forces, or the 'cultural-ecological' factors that are well entrenched in the Culture Areas. It is for this reason we see that whenever the boundaries of the regional political

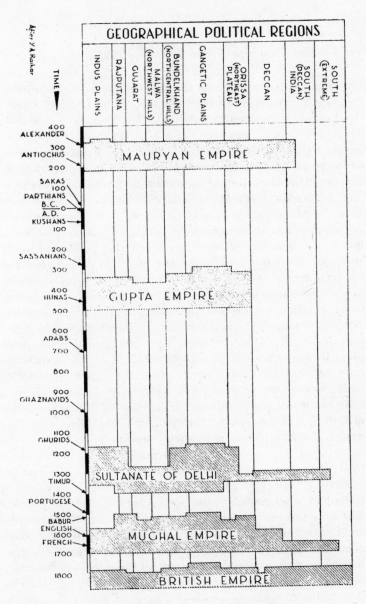

Fig. 10. *Dynamics of Indian History*

kingdoms had more or less coincided with the boundaries of the Culture Areas after the break-up of the relatively short-lived empires, the regional kingdoms had flourished smoothly. Therefore, we see that from the 7th to the 13th century A.D., during the historian's so-called 'dark ages', of the time period between the Gupta Empire and the Delhi Sultanate, the current major Indian languages and literature had developed and the linguistic-cultural boundaries which we see today were formed. However, the period was 'dark' only because historical research has over-emphasised the political aspects of Indian history. Similarly, the very genesis of the modern linguistic states is one of the most important proofs of these latent culture-historical forces, as it is the familiar pattern of the dynamics of Indian political history in which the culture-historical forces override empires and any efforts at strong centralization. The trend towards 'regionalism' was incipient during the latter part of the British rule in India, but it sought new political expression in the garb of politico-linguistic states as soon as the imposed political unity had disappeared. This reorganization took place despite the early consolidation of the British Empire over the entire subcontinent in 1858, and the introduction of certain new concepts of technological, ideological and other 'progress' which increased political consciousness.

In short, in a very generalized manner, it may be stated from the various studies carried out in archaeology, history, geography, anthropology, etc., that the 'natural' regions of India had, most probably, during the Formative Period turned first into Culture Areas, and subsequently into socio-cultural areas with their significant individuality and, still later, these areas became socio-political entities. But it must be remembered here that a formula of either environmental or historical determinism is not implied in these inferences, because the concern has been with the processual or what may be called the 'genetical' explanation of the apparent political units, or of 'regionalism', 'linguism', etc., in India today. The simple 'bird's-eye' view that is being emphasised here is that it is essential to bear in mind the long-range antecedents of any current or past socio-cultural and political phenomena of India, because of the long continuity of India's traditional society, culture and civilization.

III

An exhaustive analysis would be necessary in order to understand the reasons why culture-historical forces have defied—at least in the past—all attempts at forging either a true political unification of India or a gradual increase in national consciousness. But, perhaps, one might in brief venture to guess some of the basic reasons. Thus, for instance, India's political ideals and norms which the 'rulers' had attempted to enforce were generally based on certain religious, geographical or other abstract theoretical concepts of the unity of the subcontinent. Therefore, whenever these political ideals were put into practice, with or without force, the basic self-generating socio-cultural and socio-economic systems and institutions of Indian society were left untouched, and hence political impositions or ideologies have never broken up the essential structure of Indian society and civilization. But, as we have stressed elsewhere, this does not mean that there has been an ossification of Indian society. This means that constant socio-cultural, socio-economic and socio-political *reorganization* must always have been taking place all the while. However, whenever and whatever changes there were brought about, they were never able to break down or alter the *structural* pattern of Indian society and civilization that is present in the ancient corporate institutions at the village level. It is because of this structure, particularly at the village level, that India has been able to preserve its long continuity with the traditional past, and even the British had deliberately retained the traditional Indian institutions which they, naturally, utilized for their own political and administrative purposes.

Thus, in the context of the recent trend in India with the issue of 'regionalism', 'linguism', etc. which is being hotly and often violently debated, the long-range culture-historical view assumes crucial importance for any understanding of these problems at the political level. It is imperative to bear in mind the two sets of concrescent processes which are fundamental to the nature of Indian society and civilization. It is often stated that these various regional assertions in India today are disruptive forces, and due "to political exigencies, of late, it has become a fashion to decry the regional forces without a proper assessment of their origin and significance".[21] Frequent political references lay undue stress on India's political unity, 'emotional integration', etc., and on its cultural capacity for absorbing new elements. It is indeed true, as has been stated elsewhere, that the common systems and institutional patterns do provide a semblance of this fundamental unity. But this unity has not reached the level of a functioning 'total' entity either in the unitary cultural sense or in the sense of the modern nation-state political concept. Therefore, it is often overlooked that this political unity today is as yet somewhat at the abstract ideological level, and the equally important aspects of India's 'diversity' are often forgotten. Moreover, apart from the culture-historical aspects and language, there are other unifying socio-cultural features within each of these regional areas which have enabled them to remain as viable Culture Areas. For instance, says Karve: "Three things are absolutely necessary for the understanding of any cultural phenomenon in India. These are the configuration of the linguistic regions, the institution of caste and the family organization... The linguistic regions possess a certain homogeneity of culture, traits and kinship organization. The common language makes communication easy, sets the limits of marital connections and confines kinship mostly within the language region. Common folk songs and common literature characterize such an area... Welding of the Indian subcontinent into a nation is a great *cultural* task, but very often the urge for uniformity destroys much that from an ethical and cultural point of view can be allowed to remain".[22]

Therefore, it is crucial for social and political scientists, practical politicians, historians, etc. to bear in mind this overall and long-range view in any generalizing statements that they may make with regard to the problem of India's unity, diversity, 'regionalism', etc. The regional forces, Centre-State relationship problem, etc. are too often attributed to 'disruptive' political forces as well as to a general immaturity of the nation. But the long view suggested here will make us realize that the socio-cultural matrix of Indian civilization will most probably give rise to different political systems and institutions than those which have been handed down to us by the British. It cannot be over-emphasised that the micro-local and the macro-regional culture-historical factors must also inherently play their part. Similarly, it is apparent that all universal schemes that do not take into account the specific regional factors in India will prove to be misfits in a traditionally structured civilization like that of India.

Of course, the traditional structure of Indian society is now, in the 20th century, showing some signs of change, and of being broken up by the introduction of Western concepts and institutions such as, for instance, democracy which is an entirely new concept of state and society for India. This is new because with the introduction of adult franchise, the power now of installing, electing, political and administrative authority for the first time rests with the smallest constituent voter. This basic unit of democracy lives in an overwhelming majority in the villages, even if we exclude his counterpart in the urban and semi-urban areas for the present. He has a world-view and a 'universe' that is oriented to the traditional socio-economic and socio-structural pattern of society. Hence, it is tradition—culture-history—that educates and governs the values, attitudes and behaviour of this basic individual, and despite the beginnings of incipient industrial urbanization in India, we are far from even being termed as a 'transitional' society. Therefore, it should be quite natural to expect the loyalties of this basic unit to remain at the regional—micro-macro—level rather than at any other wider nationalistic or humanistic level (Fig. 11). Democracy in the true sense, rather than the mere 'technical' political democracy that is prevalent at present, will only become possible with the ever-widening psychic awareness of this basic unit of democracy, the individual. The means to increase this awareness are many, such as through a rapid increase of those institutions which are part and parcel of the process of 'modernization', i.e., industrialization, secular humanistic education, etc., which are spread by means of the mass communication media as television, radio, films, the press, etc. (Fig. 12). Of course, these Western institutions, which represent the 20th century concept of 'progress', have already been introduced in India. These, because they are alien to the traditional ones, are causing changes in the older structure as well as releasing both the ultramodern and conservative traditional forces. The traditional culture-historical forces are today very strongly playing their role in the form of 'revivalistic' political parties. Nevertheless, these various forces cannot be ignored and, therefore, there is an imperative need to keep in healthy balance the forces of 'unity and diversity', 'traditionalism and modernism', as one learns from India's traditional socio-cultural history, etc.

To conclude this section, emphasis has been laid on the importance of learning some lessons from the depth of culture-history, specially in a case like India where there is a

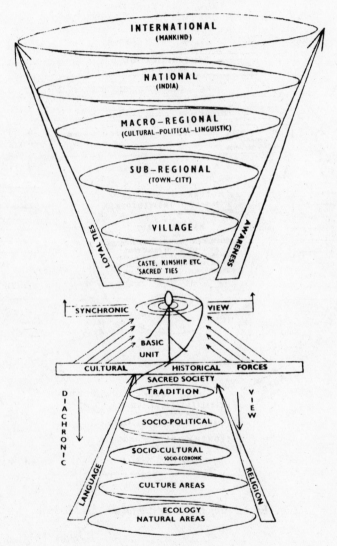

Fig. 11. The Individual, Culture-History and Awareness

175

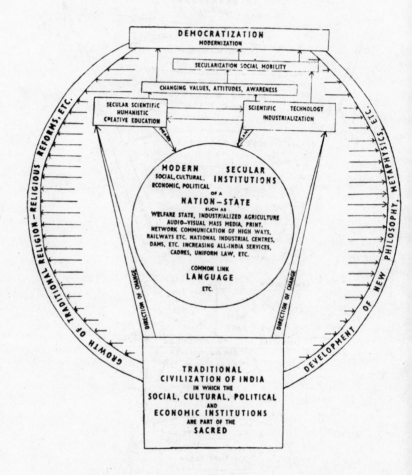

Fig. 12.   From the Traditional to the Modern

long continuity of its traditional civilization. Here, the preliterate, protoliterate and literate periods of history are of
equal importance. Therefore, the long-range view of many of
India's problems is extremely important. The brief 'digression'
with this problem of 'regionalism' was given in order to illustrate
the relevance of integrated interdisciplinary studies, and the
'use' of archaeological studies to matters of today, current
affairs. Thus, as Prof. Childe had stated: "Prehistoric archaeology has effected a revolution in man's knowledge of his
own past, comparable in scale to the revolutions achieved by
modern physics and astronomy . . . like a new optical instrument
it has already extended our range of backward vision fifty-fold
and is every year expanding the field surveyed with the new
perspective. . . With the field of historical vision thus deepened
and enlarged the sociologist should be able better to judge. . ."[23]
our own times. But any link between the prehistoric past and
modern times will only be possible if future research is carried
out in terms of the processual social science approach towards
the problems of not only archaeology but also of historic records,
folk literature and ethnographic studies.

IV

The question that now arises from the above-stated digression is, what specifically are the lessons that are of importance
for the future of archaeological research in India ? Let us,
therefore, now turn to the specific ecological approach to some
of the problems of prehistoric archaeology in India, which is
not a new one for archaeology in general. Thus, for instance,
in Europe Grahme Clark has already shown us the interrelatedness of ecological factors to the economy of prehistoric communities, and he states: "There is no more faithful indication
of regional differences of soil and climate and few which define
more accurately the limits of economic zones at different stages

of prehistory than vegetation... Since the quest for food is the central fact of economic life, it follows that plant ecology and its development must be of the utmost relevance to economic history".[24]

Hence, Indian archaeology must begin to apply certain key ecological concepts, methodology and techniques (specially cartography) which can be fruitfully utilized for the objectification, quantification, measurement and comparison of specific archaeological (palaeo-sociological or anthropological) phenomena. The first essential step in carrying out such studies in India would be to work out or agree to a 'functional' classification of the micro-and-macro regions, perhaps along the classification of the main Culture Areas that has been suggested above, because archaeological evidence must be explored and excavated within the framework of Culture Areas. The questions which may then be asked, after the micro-macro Culture Areas have been diligently worked out by archaeologists in cooperation with members of other disciplines, could be in terms of what the late Prof. Childe had suggested: "So soon as reasonable culture sequence be available the immediate task is first to clarify the economy and sociology of the constituent cultures or rather of the societies they represent in the archaeological record. What did they live on... How was the land exploited... from home-steadings, dispersed hamlets or nucleated villages?... The answer will, of course, illumine the sociological issues connected with land tenures... What sort of population density has to be reckoned with?... Note that not only for prehistoric phases but also for periods fitfully illuminated by written texts is archaeology needed for the elucidation of economic and demographic as well as technical problems... In so far as the above question can be answered a reasonable account of the culture's (i.e., the society) economy can be offered; the culture can be described as a functioning economic organization... From this basis it is worth while and indeed obligatory, however perilous,

to attempt sociological inferences".[25]   Thus, in some such manner alone will the phases of the prehistoric period tie up with the
Formative, Ancient, Medieval and the Modern periods of Indian
civilization, both regionally as well as on the all-India level.

It is, of course, easier to attempt this cultural-ecological
approach at the level of the pre-agricultural habitats because
at this stage the environment and culture are bound together
in rather close relationships.   Therefore, the ecological approach
gains greater importance for prehistoric societies since the social
system of this level of culture depends largely upon the technological and economic system which, in turn, depends upon the
fauna, and the fauna is itself dependent upon the flora, etc.
Therefore, not only is it possible but also desirable for archaeologists to identify and correlate all of these interrelated systems
within the ecological framework, while reconstructing and interpreting an archaeological 'culture' or site.   The problem which
now arises is to devise ways and means of analysis whereby
these interrelated factors may be discovered at the sites.   The
elementary unit of analysis for purposes of such archaeological
research (from the ecologist's viewpoint) is to locate the 'activity pattern' or 'activity' at a particular site.   The closest ap-
proximation to this ecological conception of 'activity' is the
notion implied by such terms as 'occupation', 'functionary units'
or 'niche', which practically designate the same meaning but
are less frequently used terms within general ecology.[26]   Hence,
in this manner of analysis the site will have to be envisioned
as a system in which there is an organization of 'activities'
(occupations) that are to be seen in an overlapping and inter-
penetrating series of "activity constellations, or groups".

But the important question which now arises, and it is sure
to arise in the mind of the traditional archaeologist, is that in
theory the problem of seeking 'activities' or 'functionary units'
may be legitimate, but in the field how is this viewpoint to be
carried out with regard to prehistoric communities ?   To this,

one can certainly admit that the difficulties inherent in such research are formidable, but these are certainly not insurmountable because archaeological research in these terms has already been initiated very fruitfully outside of India. In fact, the question may also be dismissed because it is hangover from the traditional concept of the widespread belief that not only is the scope of knowledge that is obtainable from the 'stone-age' period limited but that there is also precious little socio-cultural information that may be obtained from these 'primitive' societies. But this romantic notion of 'primitive' tribes is quite contrary to what is known not only from current theories about human society but also from the knowledge of ethnography. This romantic notion can, however, easily be refuted by giving the following ethnographic example.

This is the case of an Australian aboriginal society (the Yir Yoront) in which the simple stone 'handaxe' was related to different 'activities' even at a technologically 'primitive' level of society and had played an important role in that society as a cultural trait. The task of making the 'handaxe' among the Yir Yoront was for the adult men and was not considered appropriate for women and children. The stone axe was made by a number of simple technical skills by the men, but even this simple task had required 'activities' at several locations. "First of all a man had to know the location and properties of several natural resources found in the immediate environment: pliable wood for a handle which could be doubled or bent over the axe-head and bound tightly: bark, which could be rolled into a cord for the binding: and gum, to fix the stone head in the haft. These materials had to be correctly gathered, stored, prepared, cut to size and applied for manipulation".[27] These activities for the production of a simple handaxe were carried out within certain territorial limits. Apart from this, the axe was associated with other activities which it was itself required to produce. "The use of the stone axe as a piece of capital equipment used in producing other goods indicates its very great importance to the subsistence economy of the aboriginal. Anyone, man, woman or child could use the axe; indeed, it was used primarily by women, for theirs was the task of obtaining sufficient wood to keep the family camp burning all day, for cooking or other purposes, and all night against mosquitos and cold. . . The stone axe was also prominent in interpersonal relations. Yir Yoront men were dependent upon interpersonal relations for their stone axe heads, since the flat geologically recent, alluvial country over which they range, provides no suitable stone for this purpose. The stone they used came from quarries four hundred miles to the south reaching the Yir Yoront through a long line of trading partners. Some of these chains terminated with the Yir Yoront men, others extended on farther north to other groups, using Yir Yoront men as links (in exchange for spears). . . Thus trading relations, which maybe extended the individual's personal relationship beyond that of his own group, were associated with spears and axes, two of the most important items in a man's equipment. Finally, most of the exchanges took place during the dry seasons, at the time of the great aboriginal celebrations centering about initiation rites or other totemic ceremonials which attracted hundreds and were the occasion for much exciting activity in addition to trading".[28] The stone axe had also played an important role in the kinship relationships within the Yir Yoront society.

This brief example from ethnography, among the many one could cite, reveals that even in 'preliterate' societies technological items have to be understood in their wider socio-cultural relationship because they are associated with a great number of activities and, functionally, technological items are also sociologically and ideologically meaningful. Recently, some very important field studies along these lines have been carried out in the Euro-American context, such as by Binford. He states:

"If we view culture as man's extra-somatic means of adaptation, we must isolate and define the ecological setting of any given socio-cultural system, not only with respect to the points of articulation with the physical and biological environment but also with points of articulation with the socio-cultural environment... It is argued that the methodology most appropriate to the study of cultural process is a regional approach in which we attempt to gain reliable and representative information concerning the internal structure and ecological setting of successive cultural systems... The development of techniques for the recovery of data in structural terms is believed to be crucial, for it is the structure of archaeological remains that informs about the cultural systems, and it is the cultural system which is the seat of process... Many of the limitations of currently available data are believed to derive from the failure to sample population of activity loci within a regional universe... Consequently, our current understanding of the prehistoric past is largely in terms of style distributions and cultures defined in terms of discrete trait distributions and stylistic characteristics: this is certainly not a situation conducive to studies of cultural process".[29]

Binford and his wife have applied these concepts in quite some details to the Mousterian (Levallois facies) assemblage. The basic assumption underlying this recent important paper is well worth while for us to note: "If we assume that variation in the structure and content of an archaeological assemblage is directly related to the form, nature and spatial arrangement of human activities, several steps follow logically. We are forced to seek explanations for the composition of assemblages in terms of variation in human activities. The factors determining the range and forms of human activities conducted by any group at a single location (the site) may vary in terms of a large number of possible 'causes' in various combinations. The broader among these may be seasonable regulated phenomena, environmental conditions, ethnic composition of the group, size and structure of the group regardless of ethnic affiliation. Other determining variables might be the particular situation of the group with respect to food, shelter, supply of tools on hand, etc. In short, the units of 'causation' of assemblage variability are separate activities, each of which may be related to both the physical and social environment, as well as interrelated in different ways.

"Since a summary description (as at present) of a given assemblage represents a blending of activity units and their determinants, it becomes crucial to partition assemblages of artifacts into groups of artifacts that vary together, reflecting activities. If techniques were available to isolate artifact groups reflecting activities within assemblages, then the ways in which they are combined at various localities could be analysed. We, therefore, seek a unit of comparison between the single artifact types and the total assemblage — a unit that will, we believe, correspond to the basic units responsible for the observable variation within the assemblage.

"The major methodological problem is the isolation of these units and a comparison between these, utilizing multi-variant techniques. *Factor analysis* seemed the most appropriate method (Harmann, 1961). This technique, although widely used in other scientific fields, has not been commonly applied in prehistory. . ."[30]

It is obvious from the above ethnographic and archaeological examples that if any criticisms with regard to difficulties and the impossibility of discovering details specially about prehistoric Man are tenable, it is only because piecemeal percentage comparisons of all types are being carried out at present. This latter method by itself is of little importance for establishing 'cultural' similarity or differentiation, and is an instance of the 'naive' theoretical base of Indian archaeology because it presumes that preliterate societies were so very simple that there

was no variation within them in terms of seasonal or situation-
ally specialized variations in the pattern of group activities.
It is almost self-evident from the data of anthropology,
specially ethnography, that this is seldom the case. But this
approach should not be construed to mean that the socio-
cultural situation of the past societies was the same as it is
today.

What is being suggested is that, if we continue to follow the
principle of proceeding from the known to the unknown, which
archaeologists as historiographers as it is do follow, then the
base line for archaeological research should also be ethnographic
fact and other currently valid socio-cultural laws and generalizations. Thus, it becomes incumbent upon Indian archaeologists
to attempt new concepts and methods in their field because
'finer controls' of the data are possible. It is very misleading
to state that as more precise field procedures become available, more information will become available and until then,
archaeologists should keep 'theory' at arm's length. But by
excluding theory, it is always easy to lump together excavated
material into more generalized units. However, if archaeological research in India has to be carried out in the terms mentioned in this monograph, it will mean that both explorations
and excavations will have to be conducted within a prior well-
thought out frame of reference. Of course, this is a much more
difficult and laborious process which is easier said than done.
But there is no doubt that this line of approach is very essential
for Indian archaeology today.

In this context, a few specific examples will be given below
on how the classification and typology of the lithic and ceramic
evidence might be carried out within the broad 'functional'
framework suggested here. There is sufficient general literature
available in the Euro-American context in these terms, and the
reader can refer to these in order to further analyse the Indian
material.

The Examples

(1) *The Classification of lithic-tool assemblages in terms of subsistence economies*

In India, at present, classification of stone tools is in terms of techno-typology based on simple definitions of tools in terms of borers, scrapers, burins, points, etc. But the formal description of tools should come under such functional headings as general utility tools, weapons for hunting or war, ornaments, digging implements, wood-working tools and processing or fabricating ones, etc. This 'functional' classification will, in turn, be followed by questions related to the subsistence-economic base such as (a) the context, i.e., where they came from, and (b) how do the different stone tools — assemblages — relate to each other areally, temporally and functionally. For example, if at a site, or what may really be a sub-area, there is a greater percentage of arrow-heads than other artifacts, then it may be inferred that this sub-area was probably related to some hunting activity. It is in some such manner of seeing the functional relationships and differences which will reflect the relationship of the tool-kit to peculiar environmental situations and activities of 'task' specific-areas of different groups within the same community. Similarly, seasonal tool-kit will also be indicated by the increase or decrease of the proportion of some stone-tool items, and of the non-archaeological evidences of the increase and decrease of birds, antlers, etc.[31] In short, functional classifications will reflect not only the subsistence-economic base but also the socio-cultural systems because all institutions in a given society operate by means of material apparatus, and we know that economies are also sociologically and ideologically meaningful. Moreover, these functional units have also the advantage that they can be subjected to quantifying procedures, such as distributional and frequency studies, etc.

(2) *Some questions related to the problem of ceramic evidence as aspect of economies*

Pottery is one of the most indestructible and reliable evidences of culture and is one of the chief means of archaeological classifications. But even this important evidence is seldom subjected in India to any precise functional approach. For instance, a detailed quantifiable study of pot-form categories should be worked out in order to make it possible to ask questions which are related to the economic relationship of intrusive pottery. Furthermore, distributional and frequency studies can tell us the nature of intrusion whether it was the result of trade, exchange, or as a result of the migration of peoples or some form of an adoption from other cultures; if it was meant for trade-exchange, it would depend upon the relation between two peoples, their complementary crafts or resources, sources of conflicts, etc., because trade-exchanges are not merely functional but involve cultural borrowings as well. Pottery is not as fragile, and it has often not been considered worth while by archaeologists for exchange or trade. Thus, for example, some ceramic wares such as N.B.P. were most probably traded or exchanged because of their superior make, and probably because N.B.P. also reflected status. On the other hand, utilitarian wares may have been the ones that were most frequently exchanged because at a certain socio-cultural level of integration certain villages must have specialized in some ceramic crafts (decorated wares, etc.) which were not used for domestic purposes but were meant only for ritual purposes. The reason for this form of specialization may also be a technical one such as the availability of raw material, certain special clays, etc., which must have been needed for specific ceramic types. Technical examination of the slip or paste, etc. will reveal that the raw material was imported or came from a distant region, and this in turn will imply not only economic exchange but socio-cultural borrowings as well. Similarly, a technical evaluation (e.g. whether hand-modelling is present or the wheel is present or whether open firing is done or it is by means of an elaborate kiln) of the ceramic groups will reflect technological advance and, therefore, the economic state of a given society. Answers to such a line of investigation will thus reflect from the mere technical details of the ceramics, the economic and the socio-cultural histories of societies.[32]

NOTES AND REFERENCES

1. Fried, Merton H., *American Journal of Economics and Sociology*, Vol., 11, 1952, p. 391.
2. Yengoyan, Aram A., "Ecological Analysis and Traditional Agriculture", *Comparative Studies in Society and History*, Vol. IX, I., Oct. 1966, The Hague.
3. *Readings in Cultural Geography*, eds. Wagner and Mikesell, 1962, p. 19.
4. Ibid., p. 9.
5. Sankalia, H. D., "India", *Courses Towards Urban Life*, eds. Braidwood and Willey, Aldine, 1962, pp. 60-83.
6. Duncan, O. D. and Schnore, L. F., "Cultural, Behavioural and Ecological Perspective in the Study of Social Organization", *American Journal of Sociology*, Vol. LXV, 1959, pp. 132-146; and also Wagner, Philip, *The Human Use of the Earth*, Free Press of Glencoe, 1960.
7. Subbarao, *Personality of India*, 1958, pp. 8-36.
8. Spate, O. H. K., *India and Pakistan — A General and Regional Geography*, Methuen, 1964.
9. Childe, in *Bulletin of the Institute of Archaeology*, I, 1958, p. 2.
10. Clark, Grahme, *Prehistoric Europe: The Economic Basis*, 1952, p. 7.
11. Braidwood, R. J., *Prehistoric Excavations in Iraqi Kurdistan*, Chicago, 1960.
12. Chatterjee, S. B., "Climo-Statical Regions", *Geographical Review of India*, Vol. XV, 1953, pp. 36-54.
13. Ibid., p. 54.
14. *New York Geographical Review*, Special number on India.
15. Spate, op. cit., 1964.
16. Subbarao, op. cit., 1958, p. 21.

17. Allchin, F. R., *Neolithic Cattle Keepers of South India*, 1963.
18. *Report of the States Reorganization Commission*, Government of India, 1955.
19. Raikar, Y. A., *Indian History — A Study in Dynamics*, M. S. University of Baroda, 1960.
20. Subbarao, B., "Regions and Regionalism", *Economic Weekly*, X, 28, September 20, 1958.
21. Subbarao, op. cit., 1958, p. 18.
22. Karve, Irawati, *Kinship Organization in India*, Asia. 1965, pp. 1, 4, 16.
23. Childe, V. G., "A Prehistorian's Interpretation of Diffusion", in Wagner and Mikesell, op. cit., 1962, pp. 209-217.
24. Clark, Grahme, op. cit., 1952, p. 8.
25. Childe, op. cit., 1958, p. 2.
26. Duncan and Schnore, in op. cit., 1959.
27. Sharp, Lauristan, "Technological Innovation and Cultural Change: An Australian Case", in *Cultural and Social Anthropology*, ed. Peter Hammond, 1964, pp. 84-94.
28. Ibid.
29. Binford, L. R., "A Consideration of Archaeological Research Design", *American Antiquity*, Vol. 29, 4, 1964, pp. 425-441 (p. 440).
30. Binford, L. R. and Sally, R., "A Preliminary Analysis of Functional Variability in the Mousterian of Levallois Facies", *American Anthropologist*, Vol. 68, 2, part 2, 1966, p. 241.
31. Clark, Grahme, op. cit., 1952.
32. Shepard, A. O., *Ceramics for the Archaeologist*, Carnegie Institute of Washington Publication 609, Washington D.C., 1950; and Matson, M. R., *Ceramics and Man*, Viking Fund Publications No. 41, 1965.

CONCLUSION

There are in India, as I suppose all the world over, many different reasons why students are attracted to archaeology and among these many negative ones such as a disinclination to cope with scientific laboratory procedures and quantification, or perhaps the inability to secure seats in science, engineering and economics, etc. Still, other students take up archaeology for the sake of adventure or because of an interest in the exotic or the bizarre, which probably fulfils the desire to express their individuality. But although such factors are legitimate, yet these have not given the additional intellectual drive which is so essential for any discipline to become 'sophisticated'. It is partly as a result of the lack of these drives that archaeological reports frequently reflect more the personalities of the authors, rather than represent a comparative or generalized position which should emerge from any kind of specific studies, i.e., they are better representatives of the uniqueness of the 'cultures' which each author has described. It is for this reason why one also finds classifications, typologies, etc., in Indian archaeology which are seldom alike, and this makes it very difficult for any-one to put forth useful comparisons. But the lack of a sound theoretical framework makes many Indian archaeologists believe that as little bits of evidence are uncovered, the jig-saw puzzle will be put together automatically, or that a theory would grow out of the facts themselves and express their significance. But even a glance at the other 'advanced' disciplines clearly shows the fallacy of this argument. Therefore, has it been suggested that Indian archaeology should bring about a proper balance by shifting its emphasis from the descriptive data-gathering phase to the somewhat more sophisticated description, analysis and

189

interpretation. The 'static' approach of Indian archaeology should yield to the 'dynamic' one because the least that could be done is to keep up with contemporary research trends (Fig. 13).

In retrospect, the basic contention of this monograph has been about approaches and the methodological interest of the inquiry, in order that research in Indian archaeology may benefit therefrom. But the suggestion for the use of some of the social science models presented in this monograph does not mean that these models should be taken as set entities. This would clearly be a superimposition of theory upon 'reality'. Frames of reference, models, etc. have to be fashioned and refashioned when they no longer serve the purpose, otherwise, they may well become set entities quite like the 19th century concepts which we continue to follow in India to this day. It must also be borne in mind that no one technique or concept can compare in effectiveness to the balanced combination of all the research means. This, one hopes, will eventually come about through a process of fusion and adjustment of history, archaeology and anthropology. The effort towards the integrative interdisciplinary approach seems all the more necessary for archaeology since only scattered information about past societies is preserved in the ground, in documentary evidence, or as may be deduced from the societal and cultural forms of today. Therefore, it becomes imperative for us to bear on every possible line of evidence on each single problem of archaeology. It is only such integrated manner of research, at a certain level of interpretation, which will provide some of the ways and means of fusing together history, archaeology and anthropology. However, an effort of this kind will also create problems at the organizational level, i.e., of how to achieve the cooperation and interchange of peoples and ideas between the different disciplines; for instance, of how best and in what manner the contribution of each discipline ought to be to a common enterprise. But the impression that this statement and what has been stated elsewhere in this

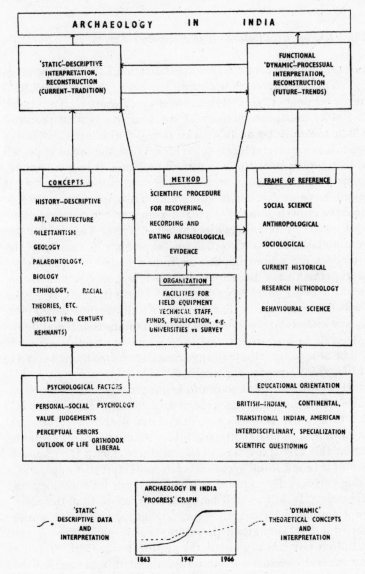

Fig. 13. Archaeology in India

monograph may create is that specialization had better be given up. This, of course, is not quite the case. Nevertheless, it is today evident that increased over-specialization has tended to isolate and neglect many of the common general problems which can only be dealt with in terms of the interdisciplinary approach. Therefore, it is to be hoped that the broad approach of the present monograph to certain problems of Indian archaeology has not been as futile, jejune and presumptuous as it might have at first sight appeared. This, since from time to time the growth of any discipline depends on the constant cross-fertilization of 'principles and experiences', and Indian archaeology today has far exceeded in 'experience'. Concepts and principles have been implicit in Indian archaeology and most explanations have been more intuitive and less systematic instead of being more systematic and less intuitive. It is also the belief of the writer that it is only within the broadened horizons of archaeology — when its research can be reduced at different levels to a science, social science and humanities — that it will be able to contribute to the understanding of human society, of life, and its needs as a whole.

However, there are bound to be misgivings and serious criticisms to these suggestions primarily because the author has had to rely on inadequate source material and literature, and he has not been able to illustrate it by actual fieldwork in India. But at this first stage, he had to rest the case with the presentation of a broad framework. Therefore, the present approach is liable to be easily exposed to the accusation of tautology and platitude. It will as well be open to criticism that the monograph implies a logical circle for, obviously, unless fieldwork is carried out to strengthen the concepts here used, there is very little that one can say about the approach put forth as well as any general conclusions. But the aim of this monograph has not been so much to present any conclusive results or any dogmatic concepts, as to suggest a reorientation of the research goals illustrated by examples. And no one will, it is hoped, regard this present monograph as more than a tentative guideline. It is also to be hoped that at least the younger students of archaeology, when supplied with such an approach, may find it of some use. The writer feels that the conceptual framework of 'function', etc., and the stress on socio-cultural processes—which in any case is implicit behind the generalized anonymous archaeological evidence—might prove to be of immense value to the growth and progress of archaeology in India. It may help to isolate and correlate a great number of socio-cultural phenomena of archaeology in a clearer perspective.

It is well known that nothing is as difficult to see as the obvious. As such, this rather obvious commonsensical and somewhat pedantic approach and discussion given in this short monograph needs no apology, for it had only become too necessary in view of the intellectually 'easy-going' way of many an Indian archaeologist (historian). He has not only not concerned himself with epistemological problems but he has even not become involved with any legitimate discussion of the minimum concepts and definitions, whether these may be original or borrowed. Hence, in this sense, the 'progress' of archaeological studies has lagged behind. In other words, the primary deficiency of theory, both before and after fieldwork, has had a 'slowing down' influence. Somehow, many archaeological reports are considered 'scientific' simply because the data they marshal are quantified by counting, measuring and giving accurate drawings. The fact is that most of the current professional archaeologists follow the straight and narrow historical descriptive approach. This may not, however, be the major reason for the lack of a development and of a greater interest in 'theory' since there are, too, the following considerations for this writer's scepticism.

(1) That there are certain implicit difficulties, over and above the scattered nature of the evidence, in the evidence of

archaeology to which it may be impossible to apply this far-fetched 'idealistic' approach of the social sciences. But this charge of the complexity and impossibility of analysing archaeological phenomena holds little validity, and is certainly not legitimate being as old as at least the Middle Ages. Archaeologists themselves are well aware that archaeological research today is able to obtain more information both through direct observation and through inference than it was possible twenty-five years ago. This 'progress' of archaeology cannot merely be attributed to the rise of 'techniques' that are borrowed from the natural and physical sciences. This has happened mainly due to the ever-widening conceptual horizons of archaeology itself.

(2) The approach of this monograph involves and demands even slower and more laborious research techniques since it calls for 'intellectual alertness' of a high order. This manner of research may entail many long years before it will become possible to present the results to the general public. It is contrary to what is possible and required today, as results have to be announced fairly early, specially of the 'sensational' finds and discoveries. The archaeologist, however, is not to blame for this state of affairs as it involves other organizational problems, specially those of obtaining funds which become easily available by such announcements of 'sensational' nature. Understandably enough, and all too frequently, those persons who are in charge of the funds, whether in public sphere or the private, are only too easily impressed by these so-called methods of sensational announcements. Without doubt it is a dilemma and its remedy lies quite elsewhere.

(3) The growth and 'progress' of Indian archaeology is tied up with the matter of 'vested' interests, apart from the one concerned with the administrative machinery of a given organization. But by this 'vested' interest is meant the present set-up of various departments, whether in the Government of India or in the Indian universities, where the research of history,

archaeology, anthropology, etc. is carried out only in specialized
'pigeon-holes', in isolation, in a set manner and in 'peace'.
Therefore, if the approach and suggestions in this monograph are
followed, it would mean the creation of disturbances in the
present research and organizational set-up of the 'entrenched'
interests. It would mean the 'dislocation', 'displacement' and
'dislodging' of those professionals who are already well 'saddled'.
Of course, this does not literally mean unemployment, but it
would certainly mean that an effort will have to be made to
wake up from the lethargy of a well-set tradition—of old values
and beliefs—both in terms of archaeology and life. Above all,
it would make those persons who are 'well-set' psychologically
reticent, defensive, i.e., the well-known phenomenon of resist-
ance to change.

Finally, it is to be hoped that the traditional archaeologist
will not be too distressed by the somewhat unorthodox approach
of the monograph, that is, if he is willing to view archaeology
in its aspect of growth. In this context, it will be only appropriate to conclude with a quotation from Redfield, and in the
light of which, one hopes, the monograph will be viewed.

"None of us can truly say that this way of work is necessarily the best way or that it either should or will prevail over
all others. All advances in knowledge is a dialectic, a conversa-
tion. To hear the relative truth of what one is one's self say-
ing one must listen to what the other worker says about what
one's self has described otherwise. The point I have striven
to make—among the many and varied mental instruments
for the understanding . . . is to be included a controlled conversa-
tion, a dialectic of opposites, carried on within one's self. . .
For understanding is increased and the needs of mankind are
met by any and all honest description, responsible to the facts
and intellectually defensible. To see what is there with the
perceptions that our own humanity allows; to render our report
so as to preserve the significance of these perceptions while

submitting them to the questions and the tests of our fellows—
that is our common duty, whatever the particular means we
take to realize it. Understanding and her apotheosis, wisdom,
are the true gods within the temple; science is not, she is only a
handmaiden, and serves with many others".[1]

NOTE

1. Redfield, Robert, *Peasant Society and Culture*, 1963, pp. 148, 168.

INDEX

acculturation process 128; of Indian Style 144-45
acropolis 82
'activities' 179
Afghanistan 82
'agency' 82, 101, 104
Agni, offering of potsherds to 129
agrarian economy of Aryans 132
Ahar 80, 89, 124
Ahichchhatra 23, 81, 125, 134
Aitareya Brāhmaṇa 132
Ajmer 82
Alamgirpur 80, 87
Alexander the Great 138, 145
amazonite 83
Ambkheri 88, 89, 126
American Indian 141
American School of Indian and Iranian Studies 23
Amri 80, 97, 112
ancient corporate institutions of villages 171
Ancient Monuments and Preservation Act 23
Andhra 89, 161, 168; Orissa Coast 159
antennae, daggers 90; swords 89
anthropological Model for Indian prehistory 49ff
anthropology, cultural 67; social 62; some concepts from 62
anthropomorphic 88
archaeological evidence, of cultural-contact situations 84, 88f; of Formative Period 77
archaeological knowledge 4
Archaeological Survey of India 18ff, 24, 34
archaeology in India 191
Aryans 37, 42, 62, 74, 106, 118, 121, 125, 128ff
Aryāvarta 145
Asiatic Society 18, 22

Assam 81; Highlands of 159
Asuras 132f
Atranjikhera 52, 88f, 124; socio-cultural interpretation of 126
Attock 90
Australian aboriginal tribes 35, 180f
authority 82, 96, 98f, 100f, 103, 105f, 116, 135
Avanti 168
awareness, and the individual 175

Babylonia 82
Bactrian 145
Badakstan 82
Bahadarabad 81, 88f
Bahal 80
Balbūth 136
Baluchistan 80, 82, 87
Banas 80, 88
Bangarh 24
baṇiā 130
Bara 52, 80, 84, 88
barbarism 34
Bargaon 88f
barley (yava) 129
bearded man of Harappa 111
Bengal 24, 81f
Bhagatrav 80
Bhāratas 135
Bhatpur 88
Bhita 22, 134
Bihar 81
Bikaner 83
binary system 123
Binford(s) 181f
Bithur 81
Black and Red Ware 88f, 124ff
Bombay 18, 83
Boston Museum 23
Brahmagiri 80, 90
Brahmanical 133f
Brahmanism 73